LADY OF WATER AND FLAME

Ancient Hymns for Tefnut

BY CHELSEA LUELLON BOLTON

Lady of Water and Flame: Ancient Hymns for Tefnut

Copyright © 2021 by Chelsea Bolton
Interior Design by elfinpen designs
Cover Design by Getcovers.com. Image of Tefnut and Tasenetnofret-Tefnut from the Temple of Kom Ombo.

DISCLAIMER AND/OR LEGAL NOTICES:
This work is not intended for financial, legal, medical, spiritual or any other advice. This book is for information purposes only.

Printed in the United States of America
First Printing, 2021
ISBN: 9798708997173
http://fiercelybrightone.com

Contents

Lady of Water and Flame

Ancient Hymns of Tefnut

The Twin Lions

The Goddess Tefnut

The God Shu

Epilogue

Dedication

To Tefnut in all Her forms and names.

Figure 1: The Goddess Tefnut.
Image from 1904. Public Domain.

Acknowledgements

Thank you to Rev. Dr. Tamara L. Siuda for granting permission to include the material from:

- Siuda, Tamara L. *The Ancient Egyptian Daybook*. Stargazer Design, 2016.

Thank you to IFAO/Le Caire for their permission to include the material from:

- Inconnu-Bocquillon, Danielle, *Le mythe de la déesse lointaine à Philae, BdE 132*, Le Caire/Cairo: IFAO, 2001.
- Sauneron, Serge, *Esna V: Les fêtes religieuses d'Esna aux derniers siècles du paganisme*, Cairo: IFAO, 1962; 2004.
- Gutbub, Adolphe. *Textes fondamentaux de la théologie de Kom Ombo*. Institut français d'archéologie orientale du Caire, 1973.
- Guermeur, Ivan and Christophe Thiers. "Un éloge xoïte de Ptolémée Philadelphe. La stèle BM EA 616". *Bulletin de l'Institut français d'archéologie orientale*, IFAO, 2001.
- Aufrère, Sydney. *L'univers minéral dans la pensée égyptienne*. Vol. 1. (Imp. de l'Institut français d'archéologie orientale, 1991.

Thank you to Holger Kockelmann, Erich Winter and the Austrian Academy of Sciences for granting permission to include material from:

- Kockelmann, Holger and Erich Winter, *Philae III: Die Zweite Ostkolonnade des Tempels der Isis in Philae. (CO II und CO II K)*, Verlag der Osterreichischen Akademie der Wissenschaften/Austrian Academy of Sciences, 2016.

Thank you to the Association Egyptologique Reine Elisabeth a.s.b.l. for granting permission to include material from:

- De Wit, Constant. *Les Inscriptions du Temple d'Opet a Karnak III: Traduction integrale des textes rituels-Essai d'interpretation.* Bruxelles : Edition de la Fondation Egyptologique Reine Elisabeth, 1968.

Thank you to Dr. Rene Preys for granting permission to include material from:

- Preys, René. *Les complexes de la Demeure du Sistre et du Trône de Rê: théologie et décoration dans le temple d'Hathor à Dendera.* Vol. 106. Peeters Publishers, 2002.
- Preys, René. "Le mythe de la Lointaine: Lionne dangereuse et déesse bénéfique." In *Sphinx: Les gardiens de l'Egypte*, pp. 141-151. Fonds Mercator, 2006.

Thank you to Rev. Tanebetheru.

Thank you to Akhytsenu and Asetmehheri.

Thank you to Dr. Edward P. Butler.

Thank you, Mom and Dad. Thank you to my family and friends.

Introduction

Tefnut is the ancient Egyptian goddess of moisture, mist, rain, clouds, water, flame and the power of the sun. She is the *Wandering Goddess* who leaves and returns to Egypt during the *Wandering Goddess* festivals on the solstices each year. As a protective goddess, Tefnut destroys the enemies of her brother, son, and father. She protects all of Egypt from harmful forces. She is an Eye of Ra, a fiery goddess, a fierce lioness, a rearing cobra, and a cat. She slays the entropic serpent enemy of the gods. Like Hethert, Tefnut is associated with women, the *menat*-necklace, the sistrum, malachite, dance, and joy. She is often depicted as a lioness and a lioness headed woman seated on a throne with the sundisk and uraeus headdress. Tefnut is the wife, sister and twin of Shu, the god of air, light, the atmosphere, and a defender of Ra.

Tefnut was created with Shu in the Primordial waters by the creator god Atum, Ra or Ra-Atum. Tefnut can also be the Daughter of Aset, Iusaaset, Hethert, Hethert-Iusaaset and Nit.

Tefnut is the Mother of Geb and Nut and the grandmother of their children. She can also be the Mother of Aset and Wesir and the grandmother of their children.

Tefnut's sacred animals include the lioness, cobra, *Uraeus*, dorkas gazelle, cat, snake, falcon, and vulture. Tefnut can be syncretized with other goddesses including Tefnut-Ma'at, Tefnut-Mut, Tefnut-Sekhmet, and Tefnut-Hethert. Tefnut-Tasenetnofret is a form of Tefnut honored at the Temple of Kom Ombo.

Tefnut is a fierce mother and protective goddess. May these pages shine some light on this enigmatic goddess.

Best Regards,
Chelsea Bolton

Figure 2: Menat with the Heads of Tefnut and Shu.
Walters Art Museum Public Domain.
Created between 664 and 380 BC (Late Period), 20th Dynasty.

Who is Tefnut?

Tefnut; Tefenet (Thphenis) is the ancient Egyptian goddess of dew, moisture, rain, mist, storms, and water. She is also a solar goddess, an Eye of Ra and a goddess associated with both flame and light. She is often depicted as a woman, a lioness-headed woman with three possible headdresses: a sundisk, an *uraeus*, or a sundisk and *uraeus*. She can also be depicted as a lioness. She can also be depicted as a rearing cobra on a staff or a serpent with a lion's head.[1] Tefnut's name translates to "That Water"; the *Tef* in Tefnut means "spit".[2] Her name can also translate to *Tef* for "spit or spittle" and *nu* for "sky water" or "rain" with the feminine –*t* ending. So, her name can be translated as "She of the Water" or "She of the Rain".

Tefnut in the Pyramid Texts

Tefnut is mentioned within the Pyramid Texts protecting the King and the deceased. In one Utterance, Tefnut purifies and protects the King.

> Heru has cleansed you with cold water.
> Your purity is the purity of Shu,
> Your purity is the purity of Tefnut.
> Your purity is the purity of the 4 House-Spirits when They rejoice in Pe.
> Be pure!
> Your Mother Nut, the Great Protectress, purifies you.
> She protects you.[3]

---

[1] Wilkinson, Richard H. The Complete Gods and Goddesses of Ancient Egypt. (New York: Thames and Hudson, 2003), 183.

[2] Tyldesley, Joyce. The Penguin Book of Myths and Legends of Ancient Egypt. (Penguin Books, 2011), 45.

[3] Faulkner, R. O. The Ancient Egyptian Pyramid Texts. (London: Oxford University Press, 1969), 150. Pt 452.

Tefnut and Shu guide the deceased in the afterlife along with Wepwawet.

> I (the deceased) have come from Dendera with Shu behind me,
> Tefnut before me and Wepwawet at my right hand.[4]

Other Utterances within the texts, describe the birth of Shu and Tefnut.

Creation of Shu and Tefnut

Shu and Tefnut have various accounts of their birth in the Pyramid Texts, the Coffin Texts, the *Book of the Dead*, the *Bremmer-Rhind Papyrus* and other sources.

Atum was an androgynous creator god at the beginning of creation. In one version in the Pyramid Texts (527), Atum masturbated and Shu and Tefnut came into being from this. In the Pyramid Texts (600), Shu and Tefnut were spat out by Atum-Khepri.

In the Coffin Texts, Shu was exhaled from Atum's nose and Tefnut was spat from Atum's mouth. Atum transfers his *Ka* (life-force) to both Shu and Tefnut through an embrace. In another version (Coffin Texts 80), Atum, Shu and Tefnut lived in the primordial waters. In order for creation to occur, all three had to become separate entities. Shu and Tefnut can also be the "male and female aspects of Atum".[5]

In another version (Coffin Texts 76), Shu and Tefnut became separated from the creator in the primeval darkness. In Coffin Texts 76, Shu says, "Atum once sent His Sole Eye searching for me and Tefnut, my sister. I made light in the darkness and it found me".[6] Atum sent the Eye Goddess to find the lost twins. Once she found them, the first

---

[4] Faulkner, Raymond O. The Ancient Egyptian Pyramid Texts. (London: Oxford University Press, 1969), 176. PT 496.

[5] Pinch, Geraldine. Egyptian Mythology: A Guide to the Gods, Goddesses and Traditions of Ancient Egypt. (New York: Oxford University Press, 2004), 63-64.

[6] Pinch, Geraldine. Egyptian Mythology: A Guide to the Gods, Goddesses and Traditions of Ancient Egypt. (New York: Oxford University Press, 2004), 64.

sunrise was created since Shu as the god of air created a void in the darkness so light could shine.

In another myth, once Shu and Tefnut were born, Atum renamed them: Shu as Life and Tefnut as Ma'at. Once named these new forms came into existence. Atum embraces both Tefnut and Ma'at.[7] The Goddess Ma'at created order in the primordial time. In the Coffin Texts, Atum said: "Tefnut is my Living Daughter and she shall be with her brother Shu; Life (Ankh) is his name; Ma'at is her name".[8]

In another account of the creation of Shu and Tefnut, in the *Book of the Dead, it* says "He (Ra) inhales Shu and he creates Tefnut".[9]

In the *Bremmer-Rhind Papyrus*, both Shu and Tefnut were created via Atum's masturbation. In one version, Atum masturbated with his hand and then put the seed in his mouth as a substitute for a womb. As he spoke, Shu and Tefnut came into being from those seeds and were "expelled from his mouth or through the nose and mouth".[10] Also, in the *Bremmer-Rhind Papyrus*, the Lord of All became separated from Shu and Tefnut. The Eye Goddess was sent to retrieve them. Once the Eye Goddess found them and the three of them returned to Atum. Once there, the Eye Goddess was enraged since Atum had created another goddess "in her place". So, in order to appease the Eye Goddess, Atum transformed her into the *Uraeus* and placed her upon his forehead.[11]

In the Memphite theology, the Ennead of Atum were created through masturbation and spoken word. The Ennead of Atum (the first nine gods) "spoke the name of everything and from which Shu and

---

[7] Pinch, Geraldine. Egyptian Mythology: A Guide to the Gods, Goddesses and Traditions of Ancient Egypt. (New York: Oxford University Press, 2004), 64.

[8] Tobin, Vincent Arieh. Theological Principles of Egyptian Religion. Vol. 59. (Lang, Peter, Publishing Incorporated, 1989), 79. Coffin Texts 80.

[9] Allen, T. G. *The Book of the Dead or Going Forth by Day*. (Chicago: University of Chicago Press, 1974), 105. Spell 130: a.

[10] Pinch, Geraldine. Egyptian Mythology: A Guide to the Gods, Goddesses and Traditions of Ancient Egypt. (New York: Oxford University Press, 2004), 63-64.

[11] Pinch, Geraldine. Egyptian Mythology: A Guide to the Gods, Goddesses and Traditions of Ancient Egypt. (New York: Oxford University Press, 2004), 64.

Tefnut came forth".[12] Once Shu and Tefnut were created, Atum's Hand became a goddess. Iusaaset or Hathor-Iusaaset is often the personification of the "Hand of Atum" or the "Hand of God". The Hand Goddess was the consort and daughter of Atum.[13]

In another story of their birth, Shu and Tefnut are born as a pair of lion cubs.[14]

Shu and Tefnut had the first sexual union and Tefnut became pregnant with Nut, the Sky Goddess and Geb, the earth god. Nut and Geb fell in love. From this union, Nut became pregnant with Wesir, Heru Wer, Set, Aset and Nebet Het. Shu separates Nut and Geb with atmosphere and there is space between Heaven and Earth for creation to continue. Nut can finally give birth to her five children.[15]

Wandering Goddess Myth

The Eye of Ra is a title and role of many ancient Egyptian Goddesses. These Eye Goddesses protect Ra and all of Egypt from enemies. The Eye Goddesses are associated with cobras, snakes, lionesses, leopards, panthers and cats. They wield magic, weapons and flame to protect all of Egypt against enemies.

The Eye of Ra is associated with the cycles of the sun, solar eclipses, the star Sopdet (Sirius), Venus, the Morning Star, and the full moon. All the Eye goddesses are associated with solar rays, flame and starlight—in both restorative and destructive capacities.[16] Tefnut as an Eye of Ra Goddess would be associated with all of these.

---

[12] Pinch, Geraldine. Egyptian Mythology: A Guide to the Gods, Goddesses and Traditions of Ancient Egypt. (New York: Oxford University Press, 2004), 63.

[13] Pinch, Geraldine. Egyptian Mythology: A Guide to the Gods, Goddesses and Traditions of Ancient Egypt. (New York: Oxford University Press, 2004), 63.

[14] Wilkinson, Richard H. The Complete Gods and Goddesses of Ancient Egypt. (New York: Thames and Hudson, 2003), 183.

[15] Pinch, Geraldine. Egyptian Mythology: A Guide to the Gods, Goddesses and Traditions of Ancient Egypt. (New York: Oxford University Press, 2004), 64-65.

[16] Pinch, Geraldine, Egyptian Mythology: A Guide to the Gods, Goddesses and Traditions of Ancient Egypt. (New York: Oxford University Press, 2004), 128-130 and 131-134.

Tefnut is one of the goddesses within the myth of the *Departing and Return of the Distant or Wandering Goddess*. Within the myth, Tefnut leaves Egypt for the Nubian desert and is retrieved by Shu and Djehuty (Thoth). She finally returns to Egypt and is cooled by an *Isheru* lake, where offerings are given to her. Once Shu or Djehuty convince her to return, she marries either Shu or Djehuty. Another version has Djehuty convinces her to return to Egypt and she transforms into the pacified goddess, Hethert.[17]

There is a *Papyrus Leiden 1: 384* which survives in both demotic and ancient Greek languages which expands on the *Wandering Goddess Myth*. In the papyrus, Djehuty tries to convince Tefnut to return, she takes various forms such as the Nubian Cat, a gazelle, a vulture and a fiery lioness.

One passage is interesting in that it demonstrates Tefnut's closeness to Shu. Djehuty knows she is angry and possibly grieving as later in the text states that she has been freed from grief. But Djehuty here knows she is close to Shu, so he asks her to swear by him instead of Ra. Tefnut even tries to say she'll swear by Ra, but Djehuty counters that she will never break a vow to Shu.

"Swear by Shu," Djehuty said.

"Make me swear instead by Ra and if you make me swear...," Tefnut replies.

"I know you will not violate an oath by Shu," Djehuty said.[18]

In another part of this exchange with Djehuty, Tefnut transforms into a fierce lioness. Tefnut becomes a goddess whose eyes and face

---

[17] Tyldesley, Joyce. The Penguin Book of Myths and Legends of Ancient Egypt. (Penguin Books, 2011), 48-51.

[18] Adapted from West, Stephanie. "The Greek version of the legend of Tefnut." *The Journal of Egyptian Archaeology* 55, no. 1 (1969): 166.

blaze with flame, whose back is colored red like blood, and whose fur coat smoke because of the flames. Her light was so bright that she shone like the "sun at noon". Her power was so great that people "feared her because of her power".

> She transformed Herself
> into Her beautiful figure of an angry lioness
> a shapely figure.
> She threw Her husband away.
> Her fur smoked from fire.
> Her back had the color of blood,
> Her face glinting like the sun's disk.
> Her eyes glowed with fire.
> Her eyes blazed like flame,
> throwing fire, like the sun at noon.
> She shined from it all.
> All who were near Her feared Her
> because of Her power.[19]

Another passage has an alternate occurrence where Djehuty is absolutely terrified of Her. With only a piercing cry, Tefnut makes the earth open up, the mountains and stones shake, the desert overflowed with sand, the mountains became charred black, and a solar eclipse happened at midday. Djehuty is so frightened of Tefnut that he gets shivers, disoriented and his strength is depleted from moving constantly as a grasshopper. Djehuty couldn't tell the sky from the earth because it was so dark because of the eclipse.

> She let out a piercing voice with the Power of Her Voice,
> Then the desert opened its mouth,
> And the stone spoke with the sand,

---

[19] West, Stephanie. "The Greek version of the legend of Tefnut." *The Journal of Egyptian Archaeology* 55, no. 1 (1969): 169.

The Mountain shook for two hours.
The Baboon (Djehuty) was greatly afraid,
In the hour, where He saw the power of Her words,
The desert covered their countenance
And mountains became black.
The sun darkened at noon
And He did not recognize the sky anymore.
His flesh was like the feverish and like a frog.
He jumped like a grasshopper and devoured his strength.
His body like that of the dwarf.
He stood on His both feet,
And had the shape of a monkey of the Sun Barque
In front of the Goddess,
With great fear
And did not know any place of the world.[20]

In another part of the text, Djehuty speaks to Tefnut while trying to convince her to return to Egypt. He calls Her "Cat", "Whispering Cat"; "of vengeance and revenge" and a "Daughter of Ra". Tefnut for an unknown reason is "freed from grief" and her heart is "in joy". She also mentions that she is disgusted by wickedness which would imply that she is not a heartless goddess who only does violent acts because she can.

I know that the Cat is Your Name.
Because She is the fiber...
Which retaliation has no power
I know She is the embodiment of death and which never dies.
You are the embodiment of vengeance and revenge,
namely the Daughter of Ra.
You are called the Whispering Cat,

[20] West, Stephanie. "The Greek version of the legend of Tefnut." *The Journal of Egyptian Archaeology* 55, no. 1 (1969): 170.

because it is She who whispers
in the ear of the earthlings.
Then She laughed, namely the Ethiopian Cat.
Her heart was cheerful over the words
Which the little dog-monkey (Djehuty) had said.
She praised him very much,
saying, "I will not kill you and do not let you kill you."
My disgust is to witness wickedness;
rather you should only do you good.
What is it that I do to you, violence,
since you did not do me any bad, but only good?
You have freed My heart from grief.
You have made it come forth in joy.[21]

Finally, Djehuty convinces her to return to Egypt. Along the way, Djehuty tells Tefnut fables, stories, and hymns. As Tefnut is returning to Egypt, Tefnut stops in El-Kab and "appears" as a vulture.[22]

Normally Tefnut or Hethert-Tefnut is considered the "Right Eye of Ra", a solar goddess and is associated with the *Wandering Goddess* myth via the sun's journey. Within the Ptolemaic Temple of Hemispeos, Hethert-Tefnut is honored as the Left Eye or the Full Moon and Nekhbet is honored as the Right Eye or the Sun during the *Return of the Wandering Goddess* Festival. Richter concludes that Hethert-Tefnut is the secondary goddess and Nekhbet is the main goddess of this region is why they are honored as the Full Moon and Sun, respectively.[23]

---

[21] West, Stephanie. "The Greek version of the legend of Tefnut." *The Journal of Egyptian Archaeology* 55, no. 1 (1969): 178.

[22] West, Stephanie. "The Greek version of the legend of Tefnut." *The Journal of Egyptian Archaeology* 55, no. 1 (1969): 181.

[23] Richter, Barbara A. "On the Heels of the Wandering Goddess: The Myth and the Festival at the Temples of the Wadi el-Hallel and Dendera." Dolinska, Monika and Beinlich, Horst (eds.) 8. Ägyptologische Tempeltagung: interconnections between temples : Warschau, 22.-25. September 2008. Germany: Harrassowitz, 2010: 168 and 172-173.

Greek Myth: Geb Rapes Tefnut

There is a late myth where the creator was in the Heavens and Shu ruled Egypt with Tefnut. Eventually, Shu lost both the throne and Tefnut to their son, Geb.[24]

This is a Greek myth, where Tefnut is imprisoned and raped by her son Geb. She is freed and Geb is punished by the Gods.

In the *Naos of El Arish*, it states that Geb tries to overthrow Shu. Geb fights, injures and kills his father. He then kidaps and rapes his mother. The rape is inferred in the text as during her imprisonment the weather is terrible and the sky darkens with rainclouds. Geb tries to steal the royal diadem of his father Shu, but the *uraeus* on the crown's brow spits fire at him. Geb is badly burned and flees. He then makes a shrine to the *Uraeus* and the goddess is appeased. The *Uraeus* goddess here is a form of the goddess Tefnut herself. She is the one who gives punishment for his crime against her. Once, Geb appeases the goddess, his burns are healed. He then becomes King, honoring the legacy of his father.[25]

The *Mythological Manual Florence p.Brooklyn 47.218.84*, says about this myth is that Geb and Tefnut "sin against" Shu. Wenut takes a spear and slaughters Geb for the crimes against Shu and because Geb was sleeping with Nehmetawai in Hermopolis and Nehbetanet in Buto. Nehbetanet here is identified with "Horit, the Great, Sekhmet in Memphis and Tefnut, in the House of Pain".[26] In another portion of the

---

[24] Pinch, Geraldine. Egyptian Mythology: A Guide to the Gods, Goddesses and Traditions of Ancient Egypt. (New York: Oxford University Press, 2004), 197.

[25] Von Lieven, Alexandra. "Antisocial Gods? On the Transgression of Norms in Ancient Egyptian Mythology," in Nyord, Rune, and Kim Ryholt, eds. Lotus and Laurel: Studies on Egyptian Language and Religion in Honour of Paul John Frandsen. Vol. 39. (Museum Tusculanum Press, 2015), 191-192.

[26] Von Lieven, Alexandra. "Antisocial Gods? On the Transgression of Norms in Ancient Egyptian Mythology," in Nyord, Rune, and Kim Ryholt, eds. Nyord, Rune, and Kim Ryholt, eds. Lotus and Laurel: Studies on Egyptian Language and Religion in Honour of Paul John Frandsen. Vol. 39. (Museum Tusculanum Press, 2015), 191-192.

text it mentions that Geb jailed and raped Tefnut. For his crime, he was sentenced by the court to lose his girdle, an object of his power.[27]

Within this myth cycle, Shu, Geb and Tefnut are equated with the gods of Hermopolis. Shu is equated with Djehuty, Geb is Djehuty's enemy Baba and Tefnut is equated with Nehmetawai.

Further in the text it mentions that Geb is forced to eat urine for this crime. It also implicitly mentions that Geb is responsible for the death of Shu. "Shu, when his *Ba* flew to Heaven from this place in front of Geb".[28] It also mentions that Tefnut is punished for being raped. Her head is cut off by Heru Wer (Haroeris) as Onuris and Geb veils his face.

Further, the text states that Onuris (Shu) thrusts his spear into Geb for raping Tefnut. The text alludes to Geb being castrated for his crime.[29]

Lastly, in *p.Salt 825*, it states that Shu kills Geb for his crime. Shu weeps after doing so and revives Geb "for his son Wesir" so that the divine royal lineage can continue.[30]

This myth is alluded to in a *Magical Papyrus London and Leiden 13:1-10.*

> As for Geb, he turns into a bull
> And mates [the Daughter] his mother Tefnut once again.[31]

---

[27] Von Lieven, Alexandra. "Antisocial Gods? On the Transgression of Norms in Ancient Egyptian Mythology," in Nyord, Rune, and Kim Ryholt, eds. Nyord, Rune, and Kim Ryholt, eds. Lotus and Laurel: Studies on Egyptian Language and Religion in Honour of Paul John Frandsen. Vol. 39. (Museum Tusculanum Press, 2015), 193.

[28] Von Lieven, Alexandra. "Antisocial Gods? On the Transgression of Norms in Ancient Egyptian Mythology," in Nyord, Rune, and Kim Ryholt, eds. Nyord, Rune, and Kim Ryholt, eds. Lotus and Laurel: Studies on Egyptian Language and Religion in Honour of Paul John Frandsen. Vol. 39. (Museum Tusculanum Press, 2015), 193. Footnote 39.

[29] Von Lieven, Alexandra. "Antisocial Gods? On the Transgression of Norms in Ancient Egyptian Mythology," in Nyord, Rune, and Kim Ryholt, eds. Nyord, Rune, and Kim Ryholt, eds. Lotus and Laurel: Studies on Egyptian Language and Religion in Honour of Paul John Frandsen. Vol. 39. (Museum Tusculanum Press, 2015), 194. Footnote 46 and 47.

[30] Von Lieven, Alexandra. "Antisocial Gods? On the Transgression of Norms in Ancient Egyptian Mythology," in Nyord, Rune, and Kim Ryholt, eds. Nyord, Rune, and Kim Ryholt, eds. Lotus and Laurel: Studies on Egyptian Language and Religion in Honour of Paul John Frandsen. Vol. 39. (Museum Tusculanum Press, 2015), 197.

This passage is from a demotic spell to separate a wife and husband. According to Verhoeven, this spell would want to invoke the separation between Nut and Geb via Geb and Tefnut.[32]

Previously, this passage was thought of to either describe Geb having sex with Nut since the word "daughter" is there indicating Tefnut's daughter. But this passage according to Luigi Prada says that this passage should read "Enemy" and not "daughter". So, it should read, "He (Geb) had sex with (the Enemy of) His Mother Tefnut".[33] This changes the meaning so that it is not talking about Nut. Depsite this, Luigi Prada states that this passage still states that Geb had incestuous relations with his Mother Tefnut. If the passage states that the victim is an "Enemy of His Mother Tefnut" then how is this about Tefnut? This conclusion on Prada's part is unclear.

In another myth, it mentions that Tefnut had an abortion. It is thought that this abortion is the result of Geb raping Tefnut. Since Tefnut does not abort her other children by Shu, von Lieven states that this abortion is most likely from Geb's rape of his mother.[34]

As a whole this myth is problematic for various reasons such as misogyny, the rape itself, incest and women's bodily autonomy. In one instance Tefnut the victim is also punished along with Geb. "The

---

[31] Verhoeven, Ursula. "Eine Vergewaltigung? Vom Umgang mit einer Textstelle des Naos von El Arish (Tefnut-Studien I)." Religion und Philosophie im Alten Ägypten, Festgabe für Philippe Derchain, Orientalia Lovaniensia Analecta 39, U. Verhoeven, E. Graefe (Hg.), Leuven 1991, 327.

[32] Verhoeven, Ursula. "Eine Vergewaltigung? Vom Umgang mit einer Textstelle des Naos von El Arish (Tefnut-Studien I)." Religion und Philosophie im Alten Ägypten, Festgabe für Philippe Derchain, Orientalia Lovaniensia Analecta 39, U. Verhoeven, E. Graefe (Hg.), Leuven 1991, 327.

[33] Prada, Luigi. "Divining Grammar and Defining Foes: Linguistic Patterns of Demotic Divinatory Handbooks (with Special Reference to P. Cairo CG 50138-41 and a Note on the Euphemsic Use of *hft* Enemy," in Jasnow, Richard, and Ghislaine Widmer, eds. Illuminating Osiris: Egyptological Studies in Honor of Mark Smith. (Georgia: Lockwood Press, 2017), 299. Footnote 110.

[34] Von Lieven, Alexandra. "Antisocial Gods? On the Transgression of Norms in Ancient Egyptian Mythology," in Nyord, Rune, and Kim Ryholt, eds. Nyord, Rune, and Kim Ryholt, eds. Lotus and Laurel: Studies on Egyptian Language and Religion in Honour of Paul John Frandsen. Vol. 39. (Museum Tusculanum Press, 2015), 185 and 187.

concept that a victim of rape is to be blamed and deserves to be killed is strongly reminiscent of opinions held in some cultures today".[35]

That being said, Geb is punished here in various ways such as being set on fire via Tefnut as the *Uraeus*, being slaughtered with a spear by Wenut, being pierced with a spear by Shu as Onuris, being castrated by Shu, being forced to eat urine, losing his girdle of power and being slain by Shu.

This myth cycle is from 1 Akhet 19 to 24.

- 17: Shu Protecting Himself from Geb
- 19: Shu's Triumph Over Geb
- 24: Geb's Resusciation by Shu for the Sake of Wesir.[36]

Von Lieven notes that it is important to keep in mind that these few texts are not how Geb was viewed normally. In all other texts relating to Geb including temple and ritual ones, Geb is the "Prince of the Gods" and he has legitimately inherited the rulership of the Earth from Shu. Von Lieven states: "This seems to be in stark contrast to the role as a usurper and transgressor against his father".[37]

Much of this myth is recorded during Dynasty 26 from the Late Period or during the Ptolemaic Period. Elements in this myth are

---

[35] Von Lieven, Alexandra. "Antisocial Gods? On the Transgression of Norms in Ancient Egyptian Mythology," in Nyord, Rune, and Kim Ryholt, eds. Nyord, Rune, and Kim Ryholt, eds. Lotus and Laurel: Studies on Egyptian Language and Religion in Honour of Paul John Frandsen. Vol. 39. (Museum Tusculanum Press, 2015), 194.

[36] Von Lieven, Alexandra. "Antisocial Gods? On the Transgression of Norms in Ancient Egyptian Mythology," in Nyord, Rune, and Kim Ryholt, eds. Nyord, Rune, and Kim Ryholt, eds. Lotus and Laurel: Studies on Egyptian Language and Religion in Honour of Paul John Frandsen. Vol. 39. (Museum Tusculanum Press, 2015), 199-200.

[37] Von Lieven, Alexandra. "Antisocial Gods? On the Transgression of Norms in Ancient Egyptian Mythology," in Nyord, Rune, and Kim Ryholt, eds. Nyord, Rune, and Kim Ryholt, eds. Lotus and Laurel: Studies on Egyptian Language and Religion in Honour of Paul John Frandsen. Vol. 39. (Museum Tusculanum Press, 2015), 196-197.

Hellenized and influenced by Greek mores and mythology. In ancient Egypt, the punishment for rape was death.[38]

Her Family

Tefnut was a part of the Ennead of Heliopolis along with Ra-Atum, Shu, Nut, Geb, Wesir, Aset, and Nebet Het.[39] Tefnut is the first daughter of Atum or Ra or Ra-Atum. She is created by being spat out of Ra-Atum's mouth.

As previously mentioned, she is the brother, wife, and twin of Shu. Tefnut is the Mother of Nut and Geb and the Grandmother of Nut's children: Wesir, Heru Wer, Set, Aset and Nebet Het. Since Wepwawet and Sobek can be sons of Nut, they would also count as Tefnut's grandchildren.[40]

Tefnut and Shu can be the parents or children of Aset and Wesir.

Shu, Her Consort, Brother, and Twin

Shu is Tefnut's brother, husband, and twin. He is the god of air, wind, atomosphere and sunlight. He is normally depicted as a man with an ostrich feather on his head or as a lion. Shu's name means "emptiness" or "void".[41] Shu, as the god of air, would be associated with scent. In the Coffin Texts, Shu's scent is described as "storm of the half-light" and the "byproduct of incense".[42] In the Pyramid Texts, the "bones of Shu"

---

[38] Reynolds, James Brown. "Sex Morals and the Law in Ancient Egypt and Babylon", in *Journal of the American Institute of Criminal Law and Criminology*. (United States: The Institute, 1915), 22-23.

[39] Pinch, Geraldine. Egyptian Mythology: A Guide to the Gods, Goddesses and Traditions of Ancient Egypt. (New York: Oxford University Press, 2004), 66.

[40] Franke, Detlef. "Middle Kingdom Hymns and Other Sundry Religious Texts-An Inventory", in Egypt: Temple of the Whole World: Studies in Honour of Jan Assmann. Sibylle Meyer, ed. (Brill Academic Publishers, 2004), 105-106. Stadler, Martin Andreas. Théologie et culte au temple de Soknopaios: Etudes sur la Religion d'un Village Egyptien Pendant l'Epoque Romaine. (Paris: Cybele, 2017), 29 and 32.

[41] Tyldesley, Joyce. The Penguin Book of Myths and Legends of Ancient Egypt. (Penguin Books, 2011), 45.

[42] Wise, Elliott. "An" Odor of Sanctity": The Iconography, Magic, and Ritual of Egyptian Incense." *Studia Antiqua* 7, no. 1 (2009): 70.

are referring to the morning mist or clouds and the "favorite son of Shu" is referring to lightning.[43]

Shu controls the wind and is associated with scent and incense. As the wind god, Shu is called "Wind of Life"[44] and "Who Has the Power to Grant the Wind".[45] He is also a warrior god, who slays the enemies of Ra and slays the entropic serpent. He is both the "Protector of His Father" and one who "massacres the enemies of His Father".[46] He is associated with the sun as the "Right Eye".[47]

Shu is associated or syncretized with various gods including Khnum-Ra, Khnum-Onuris,[48] Ptah-Shu,[49] Heru Wer-Shu,[50] Heru with the Strong Arm,[51] Heru Wer, Heru Wer in His aspect of Heru, with the Vigorous Arm.[52]

Tefnut and Shu are often paired together as the *Ruty*—Two Lions or as Shu the Lion and Tefnut, the Lioness. They can also be paired as Shu as Life and Tefnut as Ma'at or as the *Ka* and *Kat* (life-force and womb).[53]

---

[43] Faulkner, R. O. The Ancient Egyptian Pyramid Texts. (London: Oxford University Press, 1969), 70 and 50, footnote 21. Pt 261 and 222. Thank you to Dr. Edward Butler for this information.

[44] Sauneron, Serge, Esna V: Les fêtes religieuses d'Esna aux derniers siècles du paganisme, (Cairo: IFAO, 1962; 2004), 90.

[45] Sauneron, Serge, Esna V: Les fêtes religieuses d'Esna aux derniers siècles du paganisme, (Cairo: IFAO, 1962; 2004), 87-90.

[46] Sauneron, Serge, Esna V: Les fêtes religieuses d'Esna aux derniers siècles du paganisme, (Cairo: IFAO, 1962; 2004), 89 and 364-366.

[47] Sauneron, Serge, Esna V: Les fêtes religieuses d'Esna aux derniers siècles du paganisme, (Cairo: IFAO, 1962; 2004), 212-217.

[48] Sauneron, Serge, Esna V: Les fêtes religieuses d'Esna aux derniers siècles du paganisme, (Cairo: IFAO, 1962; 2004), 358-363.

[49] Sauneron, Serge, Esna V: Les fêtes religieuses d'Esna aux derniers siècles du paganisme, (Cairo: IFAO, 1962; 2004), 211-212.

[50] Gutbub, Adolphe. Textes fondamentaux de la théologie de Kom Ombo. (Institut français d'archéologie orientale du Caire, 1973), 323-324.

[51] Sauneron, Serge, Esna V: Les fêtes religieuses d'Esna aux derniers siècles du paganisme, (Cairo: IFAO, 1962; 2004), 358-363.

[52] Gutbub, Adolphe. Textes fondamentaux de la théologie de Kom Ombo. (Institut français d'archéologie orientale du Caire, 1973), 108.

[53] Sauneron, Serge, Esna V: Les fêtes religieuses d'Esna aux derniers siècles du paganisme, (Cairo: IFAO, 1962; 2004), 90. Excerpt from a hymn. Translated by Chelsea Bolton.

Lekov, Teodor. "The Role of the Ka in the Process of Creation and Birth." Journal of Egyptological Studies 4 (2015): 34.

Within creation, Shu and Tefnut became different concepts of time: "Shu is Eternal Recurrence and Tefnut is Eternal Sameness".[54] Shu represents Upper Egypt, while Tefnut represents Lower Egypt.[55]

Shu can represent sunlight, air and wind, while Tefnut represents moisture, fire and water. Many titles of Tefnut reflect her closeness with Shu:

- Divine Sister of Shu[56]
- Lion and Lioness[57]
- *Ruty*–Twin Lions of the Eastern and Western Horizons[58]
- Sister Next to Her Brother Shu[59]
- Two Children of Atum[60]
- Two Lions[61]
- Two Siblings[62]
- Who Does Not Stray From Him (Shu) to Any Other Place[63]
- Wife of Her Brother Shu[64]

---

[54] Pinch, Geraldine. Egyptian Mythology: A Guide to the Gods, Goddesses and Traditions of Ancient Egypt. (New York: Oxford University Press, 2004), 65.

[55] Labrique, Françoise. Stylistique et théologie à Edfou: le rituel de l'offrande de la campagne: étude de la composition. (Belgium: Peeters, 1992), 49.

[56] Leitz, Christian, and Dagmar Budde, et. al. Lexikon der Ägyptischen Götter und Götterbezeichnungen (LGG, OLA 129, Band 8). (Peeters, 2003), 701.

[57] Sauneron, Serge, *Esna V: Les fêtes religieuses d'Esna aux derniers siècles du paganisme*, (Cairo: IFAO, 1962; 2004), 90. Excerpt from a hymn. Translated by Chelsea Bolton.

[58] Tyldesley, Joyce. The Penguin Book of Myths and Legends of Ancient Egypt. (Penguin Books, 2011), 47.

[59] Leitz, Christian, and Dagmar Budde, et. al. Lexikon der Ägyptischen Götter und Götterbezeichnungen (LGG, OLA 129, Band 8). (Peeters, 2003), 701.

[60] Sauneron, Serge, *Esna V: Les fêtes religieuses d'Esna aux derniers siècles du paganisme*, (Cairo: IFAO, 1962; 2004), 90. Excerpt from a hymn. Translated by Chelsea Bolton.

[61] Pinch, Geraldine. Egyptian Mythology: A Guide to the Gods, Goddesses and Traditions of Ancient Egypt. (New York: Oxford University Press, 2004), 197.

[62] Pinch, Geraldine. Egyptian Mythology: A Guide to the Gods, Goddesses and Traditions of Ancient Egypt. (New York: Oxford University Press, 2004), 63.

[63] Inconnu-Bocquillon, Danielle, *Le mythe de la déesse lointaine à Philae, BdE 132*, (Le Caire/Cairo: IFAO, 2001), 39.

[64] Inconnu-Bocquillon, Danielle, *Le mythe de la déesse lointaine à Philae, BdE 132*, (Le Caire/Cairo: IFAO, 2001), 39.

Within the *Myth of the Wandering Goddess*, Shu bears the epithet *Anhur* (Onuris)—One Who Brings Back the Distant One; the Distant One here is referring to Tefnut, the Distant or Wandering Goddess.[65] In the Coffin Texts, Shu is decribed as He who "Pacified Her Who is in the Middle of Her Rage".[66] The one who is in her rage is Tefnut.

Like Tefnut, Shu was the offspring of Ra, Atum, Hethert, Iusaaset, Hethert-Iusaaset, Nit or Aset. Shu and Tefnut have children together, namely, Nut, Geb, Aset and Wesir.

Both Shu and Tefnut protect Wesir and destroy Set and his comrades.[67]

Tefnut is inseparable from Shu. They are often paired together in iconography, in temples and are named together often.

Fathers of Tefnut

As mentioned previously, during the various creation myths, Shu and Tefnut were created by Ra, Atum, and Ra-Atum. She is either created from Ra, Atum or Ra-Atum's spittle or she is created by the words spoken by the Ennead of Atum.

As an Eye of Ra, Tefnut is the "Daughter of Ra", who protects him with her flame, magic, and weaponry. Daughter of Ra is one of Tefnut's most common epithets. As Ra can be a tomcat, eagle, or lion, so too can Tefnut be a cat, female eagle, and lioness.[68] In one papyrus, there is a cat which is poisoned by a scorpion. The cat calls out to her father "Ra, come to your daughter!" He comes and heals her. This cat may be either Tefnut or Bast.[69]

---

[65] Pinch, Geraldine. Egyptian Mythology: A Guide to the Gods, Goddesses and Traditions of Ancient Egypt. (New York: Oxford University Press, 2004), 71.
[66] Pinch, Geraldine. Egyptian Mythology: A Guide to the Gods, Goddesses and Traditions of Ancient Egypt. (New York: Oxford University Press, 2004), 72.
[67] De Wit, Constant. *Le rôle et le sens du lion dans l'Égypte ancienne*. (Belgium: E.J. Brill, 1951), 118. Papyrus Salt 825.
[68] Spiegelberg, Wilhelm. *Der ägyptische Mythus vom Sonnenauge*. (Georg Olms Verlag, 1917), 28, footnote 11.
[69] Spiegelberg, Wilhelm. *Der ägyptische Mythus vom Sonnenauge*. (Georg Olms Verlag, 1917), 3.

Mothers of Tefnut

Hathor, Iusaaset or Hathor-Iusaaset can be the "Hand of God, Eye of Ra, Mother of Shu and Tefnut".[70] Within a magical text, it is said of Aset that "She bore Shu and Tefnut".[71] Aset can be the Mother of Shu and Tefnut.

Tefnut and Shu can also be the children of Nit. Here they are called the "Two Birds of Ra", yet Nit is the one who "created their bodies". Nit here is the Mother of Ra, Shu and Tefnut.

Let Tefnut
Awake in Peace, with You,
In Her name of Menhyt-Nebetuu
Two Birds of Ra being united in one Being,
She is Nit, the Divine Mother of Ra,
Who created Your bodies,
She who nourishes Your flesh with Her milk.[72]

In a hymn to Nit from the Temple of Esna, Shu and Tefnut are mentioned as her children along with Ra.

Nit, the Great, Mother of God
Mistress of Esna, Mother of Ra,
Who Created the Two Crocodiles (Shu and Tefnut).[73]

At the Temple of Philae, it mentions that Tefnut is the daughter of Nit. Here is the inscription, "Nit comes to see Her daughter Tefnut".[74]

---

[70] Siuda, Tamara L. The Ancient Egyptian Daybook. (Stargazer Design, 2016), 226.

[71] Borghouts, Joris Frans, ed. Ancient Egyptian Magical Texts. Vol. 9. (Brill, 1978), 40.

[72] Sauneron, Serge, *Esna V: Les fêtes religieuses d'Esna aux derniers siècles du paganisme*, (Cairo: IFAO, 1962; 2004), 89. Within a hymn to Khnum. Translated by Chelsea Bolton.

[73] Sternberg-El Hotabi, Heike., Sternberg, Heike. Mythische Motive und Mythenbildung in den ägyptischen Tempeln und Papyri der griechisch-römischen Zeit. (Germany: Harrassowitz, 1985), 38.

[74] Sayed, Ramadan. La déesse Neith de Saïs. (Egypt: Institut français d'archéologie orientale du Caire, 1982), 140.

xxiv | LADY OF WATER AND FLAME

Tefnut, Mother and Daughter of Aset

Tefnut is called "Mother of Aset".[75] This would mean that Tefnut would be the grandmother of all Aset's children: Heru-sa-Aset, Wepwawet, Sobek, Yinepu, Min, Amun, and Amun-Ra. There is a passage discussing Tefnut as the Mother of Aset from the Temple of Karnak, quoted below:

> Goddess, Mother and Daughter
> Mut-Tefnut-Aset
> Hand of God, Who Gives Birth to the Ennead,
> One says Tefnut, with regard to Her name,
> And certainly, She is with Her Daughter Tefnut
> Not moving away from the place which She occupies,
> One says Aset with regard to Her name as well.[76]

Bergman states that the "Daughter" here is Aset, while the mother here is Tefnut.[77] Within a temple calendar, Tefnut is mentioned as the "Festival of Aset, the Great, Lady of the Two Lands…It is the beginning of writing for her of her annals by her mother Tefnut".[78]

Additionally, Tefnut can also be the daughter of Aset. Aset is called "Daughter of Shu, Born of Tefnut".[79] Aset also has the title "Daughter of Shu and Tefnut".[80]

So Aset is both Shu and Tefnut's daughter.

---

[75] Bergman, Jan. Ich Bin Isis: Studien zum memphitischen Hintergrund der griechischen Isisaretalogien. (Almquist & Wiksell, Uppsalla, 1968), 30.
El-Sabban, Sherif. Temple Festival Calendars of Ancient Egypt. (Wiltshire: Liverpool University Press, 2000), 174.

[76] Goyon, Jean-Claude. "Inscriptions Tardives Du Temple De Mout à Karnak." Journal of the American Research Center in Egypt 20 (1983): 56-57.

[77] Bergman, Jan. Ich Bin Isis: Studien zum memphitischen Hintergrund der griechischen Isisaretalogien. (Almquist & Wiksell, Uppsalla, 1968), 30.

[78] El-Sabban, Sherif. Temple Festival Calendars of Ancient Egypt. (Wiltshire: Liverpool University Press, 2000), 174.

[79] Bergman, Jan. Ich Bin Isis: Studien zum memphitischen Hintergrund der griechischen Isisaretalogien. (Almquist & Wiksell, Uppsalla, 1968), 30.

[80] Müller, Dieter. Ägypten und die griechischen Isis-Aretalogien. Vol. 53, no. 1. (Akademie-Verlag, 1961), 29. Cited as Edfu 1: 315.

Conversely, Tefnut can be the daughter of Aset. Aset is called "She Who Gave Birth to Tefnut" and "She bore Shu and Tefnut".[81] Tefnut can be the Mother or Daughter of Aset.

Tefnut, Mother and Daughter of Wesir

Tefnut can also be the Mother of Wesir. In this passage, Wesir is referred to as Tefnut's son.

> Tefnut, Daughter of Ra, Mistress of the Gods,
> Protecting Her Son Wesir in Abydos.[82]

Here are two more passages from a Litany to Wesir naming Tefnut as the mother of Wesir. "His mother Tefnut shields him" and "Your mother Tefnut is behind you for protection".[83]

There is a passage in the *Book of the Dead*, which states that Tefnut's father is Ra which is normal for her, but then it states that the valley was created for Tefnut's Father, Wesir.

> Tefnut, the Daughter of Ra,
> feeds you with what Her father Ra gave Her.
> Fashioned for you was this valley
> at the burial of Her father Wesir.[84]

So, Tefnut can also be the daughter or mother of Wesir. Since she can also be a daughter of Aset, it is possible that Tefnut is the daughter

---

[81] Leitz, Christian, and Dagmar Budde, et. al. Lexikon der Ägyptischen Götter und Götterbezeichnungen (LGG, OLA 129, Band 8). (Peeters, 2003), 1-47. Borghouts, Joris Frans, ed. Ancient Egyptian Magical Texts. Vol. 9. (Brill, 1978), 40.

[82] Leitz, Christian. "Der grosse Repithymnus im Tempel von Athribis." In "Parcourir l'éternité", Hommages à Jean Yoyotte Bd. 2 (Bibliothèque de l'École des Hautes Études, Sciences Religieuses 156), Zivie-Coche, Christiane und Guermeur, Ivan (Hg.), (Turnhout 2012), 759.

[83] Junker, Hermann. Die Onurislegende. Vol. 59. (Hölder, 1917), 22.

[84] Allen, T. G. The Book of the Dead or Going Forth by Day. (Chicago: University of Chicago Press, 1974), 176. Spell 169: d.

of both Aset and Wesir. Tefnut can also be the Mother of Aset and Wesir.

Tefnut, Mother of Heru

Heru is said to be her son in this passage, "She Cleans Her City for Her Son Heru".[85] She is also called "Mother of God" which is normally a title given to a goddess who is the "Mother of Heru".[86] It is possible that she is a Mother of Heru.

Mistress of Women, Malachite and Joy

Tefnut shares some titles with other ancient Egyptian goddesses, such as Mut, Hethert and Aset. Some of these shared titles are: "Divine Mother"[87]; "Mistress of Women"[88]; "Mother"[89]; and "Mother of Mothers".[90] These titles emphasize Tefnut's association with women, motherhood, and the mother of creation as the "Mother of Mothers".

Tefnut also has titles which describe her association with the female genatalia: "Uterus That Causes Life in the Womb";[91] and "Vulva, Who Gives Birth".[92] Tefnut was essentially the first goddess created, the first female deity created by Ra or Atum, the first goddess to have intercourse and the first goddess to give birth as women do. Tefnut would then be a

---

[85] Kockelmann, Holger and Erich Winter, *Philae III: Die Zweite Ostkolonnade des Tempels der Isis in Philae. (CO II und CO II K)*, (Verlag der Osterreichischen Akademie der Wissenschaften/Austrian Academy of Sciences, 2016), 263.

[86] Sauneron, Serge, *Esna V: Les fêtes religieuses d'Esna aux derniers siècles du paganisme*, (Cairo: IFAO, 1962; 2004), 90. Excerpt from a hymn. Translated by Chelsea Bolton.

[87] Preys, René. *Les complexes de la Demeure du Sistre et du Trône de Rê: théologie et décoration dans le temple d'Hathor à Dendera*. Vol. 106. (Peeters Publishers, 2002), 205.

[88] Leitz, Christian, and Dagmar Budde, et. al. Lexikon der Ägyptischen Götter und Götterbezeichnungen (LGG, OLA 129, Band 8). (Peeters, 2003), 702.

[89] Inconnu-Bocquillon, Danielle, *Le mythe de la déesse lointaine à Philae, BdE 132*, (Le Caire/Cairo: IFAO, 2001), 23.

[90] Leitz, Christian, and Dagmar Budde, et. al. Lexikon der Ägyptischen Götter und Götterbezeichnungen (LGG, OLA 129, Band 8). (Peeters, 2003), 700.

[91] Leitz, Christian, and Dagmar Budde, et. al. Lexikon der Ägyptischen Götter und Götterbezeichnungen (LGG, OLA 129, Band 8). (Peeters, 2003), 700.

[92] Leitz, Christian, and Dagmar Budde, et. al. Lexikon der Ägyptischen Götter und Götterbezeichnungen (LGG, OLA 129, Band 8). (Peeters, 2003), 700.

goddess associated with women, women's sexuality, pregnancy, and childbirth.

Like Hethert, Tefnut can be associated with women, malachite, pleasure, joy, dance, the *menat*-necklace and the sistrum. Titles of Tefnut which describe this are:

- Mistress of Malachite[93]
- Mistress of the *Menat* of Gold and Faience[94]
- Mistress of Pleasure, Joy and Dance[95]
- Mistress of the *Sesheshet*-Sistrum[96]
- Mistress of Women[97]

Divine Adoratrice and Queens

Princess Nitocris I, a Divine Adoratrice and within the Chapel of Nitocris at Karnak, it says of Nitocris: "of all living, having appeared on the throne of Tefnut, eternally." Nitocris was identified with Tefnut Herself: "Daughter of Ra, She is Tefnut Incarnate".[98] Queen Nefertiti was equated with the goddess Tefnut just as King Akhenaten was equated with the god Shu.[99] Queen Tiye may have also been equated with the goddess Tefnut through the "Syrian Sphinx"—the sphinx with

[93] Leitz, Christian, and Dagmar Budde, et. al. <u>Lexikon der Ägyptischen Götter und Götterbezeichnungen (LGG, OLA 129, Band 8)</u>. (Peeters, 2003), 702.
[94] Leitz, Christian, and Dagmar Budde, et. al. <u>Lexikon der Ägyptischen Götter und Götterbezeichnungen (LGG, OLA 129, Band 8)</u>. (Peeters, 2003), 702.
[95] Leitz, Christian, and Dagmar Budde, et. al. <u>Lexikon der Ägyptischen Götter und Götterbezeichnungen (LGG, OLA 129, Band 8)</u>. (Peeters, 2003), 701.
[96] Leitz, Christian, and Dagmar Budde, et. al. <u>Lexikon der Ägyptischen Götter und Götterbezeichnungen (LGG, OLA 129, Band 8)</u>. (Peeters, 2003), 702.
[97] Leitz, Christian, and Dagmar Budde, et. al. <u>Lexikon der Ägyptischen Götter und Götterbezeichnungen (LGG, OLA 129, Band 8)</u>. (Peeters, 2003), 702.
[98] <u>Joyful in Thebes: Egyptological Studies in Honor of Betsy M. Bryan</u>. (United States: Lockwood Press, 2015), 160.
[99] <u>Joyful in Thebes: Egyptological Studies in Honor of Betsy M. Bryan</u>. (United States: Lockwood Press, 2015), 159. Mancini, Mattia. "Tefnut l'eliopolitana ad Amarna." *Egitto e Vicino Oriente* 39 (2016): 50 and 53.

the female head, the lion's body and wings—may be a symbol of Queen Tiye being equated with Tefnut.[100]

Mistress of the Books

Tefnut is also a goddess associated with books and the scrolls read during ritual. Therefore, perhaps Tefnut is associated with religious writing, reading and recitation of the ancient Egyptian temple priestesses, priests, chantresses and students.

Tefnut is also called the "Powerful Seshat".[101] Being associated with the goddess Seshat, would also emphasize both goddesses's association with books, writing, religious documents and festival scrolls.

Tefnut had the titles:

- Mistress of the Books[102]
- Mistress Who Reads the Festival Scroll[103]

Divine Mother and Protective Goddess

Tefnut is called both a "Divine Mother" and one "Who Slaughters Enemies". She is the "Mistress of All the Gods" as well as the slayer of enemies. She cares and protects as a mother and destroys evil forces as a protective goddess.

> Tefnut, Daughter of Ra, Mistress of All the Gods,
> Divine Mother, Who resides in Iatdi,
> Whose flame is great against Set,

---

[100] Mancini, Mattia. "Tefnut l'eliopolitana ad Amarna." *Egitto e Vicino Oriente* 39 (2016): 46.

[101] Piehl, Karl. Inscriptions hiéroglyphiques recueillies en Égypte. (Germany: n.p., 1890), 64.

[102] Kaper, Olaf E., and Oe Kaper. The Egyptian God Tutu: a study of the sphinx-god and master of demons with a corpus of monuments. (Peeters Publishers, 2003), 63. Footnote 37.

[103] Leitz, Christian, and Dagmar Budde, et. al. Lexikon der Ägyptischen Götter und Götterbezeichnungen (LGG, OLA 129, Band 8). (Peeters, 2003), 702.

who reaches the members of Her opponents,
Who slaughters the enemies of the House of the Sistrum.[104]

Tefnut also attacks the entropic serpent enemy of the Gods.

Tefnut, Daughter of Ra, Who Fulfills Her Brother's Wish,
Apep Burns with Her Glowing Breath.[105]

Underworld Goddess

Tefnut is also associated with the dead. In the *Book of the Dead*, Tefnut's waters nourish the deceased: "Wesir N drink the water of Tefnut".[106] One of her titles is "Great One of the Underworld".[107] Tefnut is also depicted as one of the judges in the Hall of the Two Truths in the afterlife. This would give her a role as a goddess of the dead.

Her Cult Centers

I have ascended to you
with the Great One behind me
and [my] purity before me:
I have passed by Tefnut,
even while Tefnut was purifying me,
and indeed, I am a priest, the son of a priest in this temple."[108]

---

[104] Preys, René. *Les complexes de la Demeure du Sistre et du Trône de Rê: théologie et décoration dans le temple d'Hathor à Dendera*. Vol. 106. (Peeters Publishers, 2002), 205.

[105] Leitz, Christian. "Der grosse Repithymnus im Tempel von Athribis." In <u>"Parcourir l'éternité", Hommages à Jean Yoyotte Bd. 2 (Bibliothèque de l'École des Hautes Études, Sciences Religieuses 156)</u>, Zivie-Coche, Christiane und Guermeur, Ivan (Hg.), (Turnhout 2012), 766.

[106] Allen, T. G. <u>The Book of the Dead or Going Forth by Day</u>. (Chicago: University of Chicago Press, 1974), 151. Spell 152: b.

[107] Leitz, Christian, and Dagmar Budde, et. al. <u>Lexikon der Ägyptischen Götter und Götterbezeichnungen (LGG, OLA 129, Band 8)</u>. (Peeters, 2003), 698.

[108] Hays, Harold M. "Between identity and agency in ancient Egyptian ritual." Nyord R, Kyolby A (ed.). Leiden, 2009: University Repository: Archaeopress: 27. hdl:1887/15716. Rite 25 from Moret, Le Rituel de Cult, Paris 1902.

Tefnut is asked to "cleanse" the King of "impurities" in a prayer.[109] At Karnak, Tefnut along with Shu, Atum, Geb, Montu and Amun were asked to grant the King strength, life and vitality.[110]

Her cult centers were Memphis, Leontopolis and Heliopolis. She was honored at Abydos, Philae and Karnak as well. The Temples of Shu and Tefnut in Heliopolis were called Both Eyes in *Menset*.[111] Tefnut and Shu were honored as a pair of lions in Leontopolis.[112]

At the Temple of Kom Ombo, Tefnut or Tefnut-Tasenetnofret (Tefnut, the Good Sister; a specialized form of Tefnut) was the consort of the sky god, Heru Wer (Horus, the Elder) with their son, Panebtawy (Lord of the Two Lands). Heru Wer was sometimes identified with Shu to form Heru-Shu.[113]

Syncretisms

Like most ancient Egyptian deities, Tefnut had syncretic forms with other gods. Syncretic gods are two or more deities who merge to form a third composite deity. Her syncretisms were Tefnut-Sekhmet, Tefnut-Bast, Tefnut-Nebetuu, Tefnut-Mut, Tefnut-Hethert, Tefnut-Hethert-Mut, Tefnut-Tasenetnofret, Tefnut-Ma'at, Tefnut-Mehit, Tefnut-Meskhenet, Tefnut-Pakhet, Tefnut-Renenutet, Tefnut-Repyt, Tefnut-Raettawy and Tefnut-Weret Hekau.[114]

[109] Meeks, Dimitri and Christine Farvard-Meeks. Daily Life of the Egyptian Gods. Translated by G. M. Goshgarian. (Ithaca: Cornell University Press, 1996), 129.
[110] Meeks, Dimitri and Christine Farvard-Meeks. Daily Life of the Egyptian Gods. Translated by G. M. Goshgarian. (Ithaca: Cornell University Press, 1996), 129.
[111] Siuda, Tamara L. The Ancient Egyptian Daybook. (Stargazer Design, 2016), 155.
[112] Wilkinson, Richard H. The Complete Gods and Goddesses of Ancient Egypt. (New York: Thames and Hudson, 2003), 183.
[113] Gaber, Amr. "The Central Hall in the Egyptian Temples of the Ptolemaic Period." (PhD diss., Durham University, 2009), 139-140.
[114] Leitz, Christian, and Dagmar Budde, et. al. Lexikon der Ägyptischen Götter und Götterbezeichnungen (LGG, OLA 129, Band 8). (Peeters, 2003), 702. De Wit, Constant. Le rôle et le sens du lion dans l'Égypte ancienne. (Belgium: E.J. Brill, 1951), 330.

Tefnut-Sekhmet

Sekhmet is connected to Tefnut through the *Return of the Wandering Goddess Myth*. There is a composite deitiy Tefnut-Sekhmet or Sekhmet-Tefnut. Both Sekhmet and Tefnut are depicted as lioness-headed goddesses with the *uraeus* and sundisk. Both goddesses are associated with flame, sunlight, slaughtering enemies, protection, magic, and destroying evil.

A hymn from the Temple of Philae connects these two goddesses:

> Tefnut, Daughter of Ra in Senmet,
> Venerable,
> *Uraeus* of Heruakhety,
> Flame,
> Powerful,
> Regent of the Spirits and Emissaries
> One who consumes the enemies
> with the burning breath of Her mouth,
> At this place,
> Her majesty returns to the land of the Pure Place,
> One who burns Apep with Her flame,
> As long as Sekhmet is Powerful in Senmet
> Burning enemies with Her burning breath
> She will burst like flame to the sky,
> Then Her name will be Sopdet.[115]

And here is another hymn with Sekhmet being called Tefnut.

> Sekhmet, the Great,
> Tefnut in Senmet,
> Who unites with Her brother,
> Who Causes *Bau* to Flourish (Shu),

---

[115] Inconnu-Bocquillon, Danielle, *Le mythe de la déesse lointaine à Philae, BdE 132*, (Le Caire/Cairo: IFAO, 2001), 83.

In the Abaton.[116]

Tefnut-Sekhmet has a connection to Shu as her brother, the one who unites with her brother and even with one of Shu's epithets, "Who Causes the *Bau* to Flourish".[117]

Tefnut-Bast

There is an inscription connecting Tefnut and Bast. Both goddesses are lionesses, Eyes of Ra, and goddesses of joy, women, beauty, fertility, and protection. Both are goddesses within the *Wandering Goddess Myth*.

Tefnut, Daughter of Ra, on the Abaton
Bast, Mistress of Philae, who came from Nubia.[118]

Tefnut-Hethert

Hethert is depicted as a beautiful woman with the sundisk in between cown horns with an *uraeus* or as a lioness-headed woman or a lioness. Hethert is connected to Tefnut through the *Return of the Wandering Goddess Myth*. There is a syncretic deity Tefnut-Hethert or Hethert-Tefnut.

Tefnut and Hethert share the titles: "Mistress of Women"[119]; "Mother"[120]; and "Mother of Mothers".[121] Like Hethert, Tefnut also has titles which tell of her life-giving powers of the female genatalia.

---

[116] Inconnu-Bocquillon, Danielle, *Le mythe de la déesse lointaine à Philae, BdE 132*, (Le Caire/Cairo: IFAO, 2001), 119. Thank you to Rev. Dr. Tamara L. Siuda for her help with this translation.

[117] Inconnu-Bocquillon, Danielle, *Le mythe de la déesse lointaine à Philae, BdE 132*, (Le Caire/Cairo: IFAO, 2001), 119. Thank you to Rev. Dr. Tamara L. Siuda for her help with this translation.

[118] De Wit, Constant. *Le rôle et le sens du lion dans l'Égypte ancienne.* (Belgium: E.J. Brill, 1951), 330.

[119] Leitz, Christian, and Dagmar Budde, et. al. Lexikon der Ägyptischen Götter und Götterbezeichnungen (LGG, OLA 129, Band 8). (Peeters, 2003), 702.

[120] Inconnu-Bocquillon, Danielle, *Le mythe de la déesse lointaine à Philae, BdE 132*, (Le Caire/Cairo: IFAO, 2001), 23.

Like Hethert, Tefnut can be associated with women, malachite, the sistrum, the *menat* necklace, pleasure, joy and dance. They are both Eyes of Ra and lionesses.

This is shown in Tefnut's titles below:

- Mistress of Malachite[122]
- Mistress of the *Menat* of Gold and Faience[123]
- Mistress of Pleasure, Joy and Dance[124]
- Mistress of the *Sesheshet*-Sistrum[125]
- Mistress of Women[126]

There is a Tefnut-Hethert-Mut syncretism as well.

Thenent-Hethert as Tefnut

The goddess Hethert or Thenent-Hethert was identified with Tefnut. Thenent was the female counterpart of the war god, Montu.

Thenent-Hethert in Armant is Tefnut
On the forehead of Ra, the August
the Mighty One in Edfu
the Lady of Heaven, the Mistress of All Gods.[127]

---

[121] Leitz, Christian, and Dagmar Budde, et. al. <u>Lexikon der Ägyptischen Götter und Götterbezeichnungen (LGG, OLA 129, Band 8).</u> (Peeters, 2003), 700.

[122] Leitz, Christian, and Dagmar Budde, et. al. <u>Lexikon der Ägyptischen Götter und Götterbezeichnungen (LGG, OLA 129, Band 8).</u> (Peeters, 2003), 702.

[123] Leitz, Christian, and Dagmar Budde, et. al. <u>Lexikon der Ägyptischen Götter und Götterbezeichnungen (LGG, OLA 129, Band 8).</u> (Peeters, 2003), 702.

[124] Leitz, Christian, and Dagmar Budde, et. al. <u>Lexikon der Ägyptischen Götter und Götterbezeichnungen (LGG, OLA 129, Band 8).</u> (Peeters, 2003), 701.

[125] Leitz, Christian, and Dagmar Budde, et. al. <u>Lexikon der Ägyptischen Götter und Götterbezeichnungen (LGG, OLA 129, Band 8).</u> (Peeters, 2003), 702.

[126] Leitz, Christian, and Dagmar Budde, et. al. <u>Lexikon der Ägyptischen Götter und Götterbezeichnungen (LGG, OLA 129, Band 8).</u> (Peeters, 2003), 702.

[127] El-Tonssy, Mohamed A. "The Goddess Rattawy in the Greco-Roman Temples" الإلهة رعت تاوى فى معابد العصر اليونانى الرومانى. *The Conference Book of the General Union of Arab Archeologists.* 15. (2012), pp. 195.

And another inscription identifies Hethert with Tefnut as a daughter of Ra nd whose plants are hidden in secret.

> Thenent-Hethert in Dendera and Armant
> is Tefnut, the Great Daughter of Ra
> whose plans are hidden in El-Tod.[128]

One inscription identifies Tefnut with Thenent only.

> She is Tefnut, Daughter of Ra in the Nome of the Beginning
> Her body is hidden more than the Gods.[129]

Tefnut-Tasenetnofret (Tefnut-Tasenetneferet)

Tasenetnofret means "Good/Beautiful Sister" and is the Wife of Heru Wer (Haroeris) and Mother of Panebtawy (Lord of the Two Lands) in the Temple of Kom Ombo. Tefnut-Tasenetnofret is depicted as a beautiful woman with the vulture headdress, a modius crown with a circlet of *uraeii*, and a sundisk in between two cow horns. Tasenetnofret is a localized form of Tefnut or Hethert at Kom Ombo.

The texts of Kom Ombo state that Tefnut settled in Kom Ombo and turned from the raging lioness into Tasenetnofret.

Tefnut came to this hill with her brother Shu when she returned from Bugem. She established herself in this nome while Ra was with and Djehuty was following her to appease her with her brother.

So Djehuty said to this goddess: You will be fine in this nome and for that we say Good Sister is the name of Tefnut in this place.[130]

---

[128] El-Tonssy, Mohamed A. "The Goddess Rattawy in the Greco-Roman Temples" الإلهة رعت تاوى فى معابد العصر اليونانى الرومانى. *The Conference Book of the General Union of Arab Archeologists.* 15. (2012), pp. 195.

[129] El-Tonssy, Mohamed A. "The Goddess Rattawy in the Greco-Roman Temples" الإلهة رعت تاوى فى معابد العصر اليونانى الرومانى. *The Conference Book of the General Union of Arab Archeologists.* 15. (2012), pp. 195.

This myth is why Tefnut is called the Good Sister (Tasenetnofret) at the Kom Ombo Temple. It is related to the *Return of the Wandering Goddess myth*. Tefnut settles down in Kom Ombo with her brother Shu.[131]

Tefnut-Tasenetnofret has many titles from the Temple of Kom Ombo and other sources. These titles describe her with many similar attributes to both Tefnut and Hethert. Tefnut-Tasenetnofret is an Eye of Ra, a goddess of sunlight, love and power. She is a protector of her father, Ra and one who saves and unites with her brother (Shu). She is an *Uraeus* and one who is the Great of Magic when protecting Ra.[132]

Tefnut-Ma'at

Both Shu and Tefnut were created by Atum. Atum renamed them: Shu as Life and Tefnut as Ma'at. Once named both Ma'at and Life came into being. Now the primordial time had order and balance of Ma'at. The Tefnut-Ma'at syncretism comes out of this.

Tefnut-Mut

Like Mut, Tefnut is called the "Venerable Vulture".[133] There is a Tefnut-Mut attested in the Ptolemaic Period.[134] Here is an inscription linking Mut with Tefnut:

Mut, Eye of Ra
Tefnut in Senmet.[135]

[130] Preys, René. "Le mythe de la Lointaine: Lionne dangereuse et déesse bénéfique." In *Sphinx: Les gardiens de l'Egypte*, pp. 148. Fonds Mercator, 2006.

[131] Preys, René. "Le mythe de la Lointaine: Lionne dangereuse et déesse bénéfique." In *Sphinx: Les gardiens de l'Egypte*, pp. 148. Fonds Mercator, 2006.

[132] Leitz, Christian, and Dagmar Budde, et. al. Lexikon der Ägyptischen Götter und Götterbezeichnungen (LGG, OLA 129, Band 8). (Peeters, 2003), 693-695.

[133] Leitz, Christian, and Dagmar Budde, et. al. Lexikon der Ägyptischen Götter und Götterbezeichnungen (LGG, OLA 129, Band 8). (Peeters, 2003), 700.

[134] Lesko, Barbara. The Great Goddesses of Egypt. (Oklahoma: University of Oklahoma Press, 1999), 150.

Tefnut-Nebetuu (Tefnut-Nebtu)

There is a Tefnut-Nebetuu syncretism. Nebetuu is a goddess whose name means "Lady of the Primoridal Time". There is a Feast of Tefnut-Nebetuu and a Chronokrater Day for Tefnut, Lady of the Primordial Time.[136] There is a Procession of Nebetuu as Hethert-Tefnut.[137]

There is a title of Tefnut "in Her Name of Mehnyt-Nebetuu".[138]

Tefnut-Meskhenet

There is a Tefnut-Meskhenet syncretism. Meskhenet is the Birth Goddess, the midwife, the protector of pregnant women and children. Tefnut was the first goddess to have sex in the traditional way and give birth as any goddess or woman would. She was the first pregnant goddess, the first mother and was the first goddess to give birth. Given this, perhaps Tefnut-Meskhenet can be a protective goddess called upon during childbirth.

Tefnut-Pakhet

I have appeared as Pakhet the Great,
whose eyes are keen and whose claws are sharp,
the lioness who sees and catches by night.[139]

Pakhet (She Who Scratches) was a goddess who was depicted with the head of a lioness with a solar disk headdress. She was called the "Lady of Speos Artemidos (Cave of Artemis)", which was a rock temple

---

[135] Marín, Antonio Hernández. "Las inscripciones de Mut en el templo de Debod." *Boletín de la Asociación Española de Egiptología* 10 (2000): 186.

[136] Siuda, Tamara L. The Ancient Egyptian Daybook. (Stargazer Design, 2016), 54 and 97.

[137] Siuda, Tamara L. The Ancient Egyptian Daybook. (Stargazer Design, 2016), 114 and 115.

[138] Sauneron, Serge, *Esna V: Les fêtes religieuses d'Esna aux derniers siècles du paganisme,* (Cairo: IFAO, 1962; 2004), 89. Within a hymn to Khnum. Translated by Chelsea Bolton.

[139] Coffin Texts 470. Faulkner translation.

for Pakhet from the time of Hatshepsut. The Greeks identified Pakhet with the goddess Artemis.

She had such epithets as "She is in the Middle of Sacred Places"; "Mistress of Heaven"; "Mistress of the Gods" and "Who is Above All Gods".[140] Her other titles have to do with being a huntress at night and a fierce lioness:

- Butcher
- Mistress of Sight
- Mistress of the Torch
- Sighted Lioness
- Who Seizes the Prey in the Dark
- With Sharp Eyes
- With Sharp Claws[141]

Two other places Pakhet was honored were, "Lady of *Wbn* (in 8th Upper Egyptian Nome)" and "She Who is in the Middle of Wadi".[142] Pakhet was associated with Tefnut because they are both protective goddesses and lionesses. Both goddesses have sharp claws and keen eyes. Both are associated with magic as "She with Great Magic Power".[143]

Tefnut-Mehit

The lioness headed goddess Mehit was an Eye of Ra, a protective goddess, a solar goddess and a Daughter of Ra. They are connected through the *Myth of the Wandering Goddess*. Mehit was paired with Anhur (Onuris), a hunting deity whose name means "He who brings back the

---

[140] Leitz, Christian, and Dagmar Budde, et. al. Lexikon der Ägyptischen Götter und Götterbezeichnungen (LGG, OLA 129, Band 8). (Peeters, 2003), 203.

[141] Leitz, Christian, and Dagmar Budde, et. al. Lexikon der Ägyptischen Götter und Götterbezeichnungen (LGG, OLA 129, Band 8). (Peeters, 2003), 203.

[142] Leitz, Christian, and Dagmar Budde, et. al. Lexikon der Ägyptischen Götter und Götterbezeichnungen (LGG, OLA 129, Band 8). (Peeters, 2003), 203.

[143] Leitz, Christian, and Dagmar Budde, et. al. Lexikon der Ägyptischen Götter und Götterbezeichnungen (LGG, OLA 129, Band 8). (Peeters, 2003), 203.

distant one". Anhur was a praise name for Shu. So, Tefnut was associated with Mehit. At Kom Ombo, Anhur was assimilated to Shu and Mehit was a form of Tefnut.[144]

According to Pinch, Shu and Tefnut could represent the sun and the moon, respectively. Mehit and Tefnut here could represent the full moon. As the *Wandering Goddess* returns from Nubia, the full moon is restored. The yearly cycle of the sun is like the yearly cycle of the moon. As the goddess returns, both the sun and moon are restored. The Left Eye symbolized the moon as the Right Eye of Ra symbolized the sun; thus, both were restored.[145]

Tefnut-Renenutet

Renenutet was the snake-headed harvest goddess in the Fayyum. Both Renenutet and Tefnut are protective goddesses associated with the *Uraeus* and cobra.

Tefnut-Repyt (Tefnut-Repit)

Repyt means "the Lady". Repyt was the wife of Min and was a lioness-headed goddess. Tefnut may have been syncretized with Repyt due to their shared lioness association.

Tefnut-Raettawy (Tefnut-Raet)

Tefnut was identified with the goddess, Raettawy. Her name means "Female Ra of the Two Lands". She was the wife of Montu and was the female counterpart to the male god, Ra. She was the creator goddess, the primordial goddess, the goddess of motherhood, the warrior goddess, the goddess of sunlight and the fierce Eye of Ra goddess.

---

[144] De Wit, Constant. *Le rôle et le sens du lion dans l'Égypte ancienne.* (Belgium: E.J. Brill, 1951), 121.

[145] Pinch, Geraldine, <u>Egyptian Mythology: A Guide to the Gods, Goddesses and Traditions of Ancient Egypt</u>, (New York: Oxford University Press, 2004), 71-73 and 177.

She was depicted as a beautiful woman with the crown of the cow horns, sundisk and two plumes. In some inscriptions Raettawy is called Tefnut.

> Raettawy in El-Tod is Tefnut
> Upon the forehead of Ra to protect His majesty with spells.[146]

Tefnut-Weret Hekau

Weret Hekau was the goddess whose name means "Female Great of Magic". This name was a title of many goddesses and a goddess herself. Weret Hekau was depicted as a snake headed goddess or a lioness headed goddess.

Tefnut had the title "Great of Magic" (Weret Hekau).[147] Tefnut-Tasenetnofret was also associated with Weret Hekau and even had the title "With Great Magic on the Head of Her Father".[148]

Conclusion

Tefnut is the first goddess created by Atum or Ra. She is the sister and wife of Shu. She is the Mother of Nut, Geb, Heru, Aset and Wesir. She is the Eye of Ra goddess appeased with offerings, the *menat*-necklace and sistrum in the *Isheru* lakes of temples. She is the goddess of rain, water, moisture and mist. She is the goddess of dance, joy, malachite and women. She is the fiery lioness, rearing cobra and stealthy cat. She is a primordial goddess, a fierce protector, a beloved wife, a beloved mother, a loyal daughter and a joyous goddess, who answers the prayers of her devotees.

---

[146] El-Tonssy, Mohamed A. "The Goddess Rattawy in the Greco-Roman Temples" الإلهة رعت تاوى فى معابد العصر اليونانى الرومانى. *The Conference Book of the General Union of Arab Archeologists*. 15. (2012), pp. 201.

[147] Leitz, Christian, and Dagmar Budde, et. al. <u>Lexikon der Ägyptischen Götter und Götterbezeichnungen (LGG, OLA 129, Band 8)</u>. (Peeters, 2003), 702.

[148] Leitz, Christian, and Dagmar Budde, et. al. <u>Lexikon der Ägyptischen Götter und Götterbezeichnungen (LGG, OLA 129, Band 8)</u>. (Peeters, 2003), 694 and 695.

Figure 3: The Goddess Tefnut in the Weighing of the Heart scene
from the Book of the Dead.
Photographed by the British Museum. Public Domain.

ANCIENT HYMNS OF TEFNUT

TEMPLE OF ESNA

AWAKENING HYMN TO SHU AND TEFNUT

Awaken in Peace!
Shu and Tefnut
Awaken in Peace!
Awaken Peacefully!
May the Two Birds of Ra
Awaken in Peace!
Awaken Peacefully!
May the Two Children of Atum
Awaken in Peace!
Awaken Peacefully!
Awake, the Two Children as Eyes
In Peace, Awaken Peacefully!
Let the Lion and Lioness, Awaken!
Ancestor Gods
Son of Tatenen, Born of Ra
Atum and His Two Birds
Flood together with the Grassland
In their names of Khnum and Nebetuu
the Great Gods who are Your *Ka*
United with Your bodies
Let the Mother of God awaken
Peaceful with You
And She does not depart from You
Ever![149]

---

[149] Sauneron, Serge, *Esna V: Les fêtes religieuses d'Esna aux derniers siècles du paganisme*, (Cairo: IFAO, 1962; 2004), 90. Excerpt from a hymn. Translated by Chelsea Bolton.

EXCERPT HYMN OF SHU AND TEFNUT

Awaken, beautifully, in peace
Shu, the Great
At the Head of Heliopolis
Wind of Life inside everything.
Let Tefnut
Awake in Peace, with You
In Her name of Menhyt-Nebetuu
Two Birds of Ra being united in one Being
She is Nit, the Divine Mother of Ra
Who created Your bodies
It is She who nourishes Your flesh with Her milk
Awaken in Peace
Awaken.[150]

---

[150] Sauneron, Serge, *Esna V: Les fêtes religieuses d'Esna aux derniers siècles du paganisme*, (Cairo: IFAO, 1962; 2004), 89. Within a hymn to Khnum. Translated by Chelsea Bolton.

TEMPLE OF PHILAE

HYMN OF TEFNUT

Tefnut, Daughter of Ra
Who resides in Senmet
Lady of the Flame in the Castle of Flame
Queen of Upper and Lower Egypt
Female Ra, Regent of the Two Lands
Great Sovereign in the Chapel
August and Powerful, Who springs from Kenset
Who attends Senmet in the form of the Venerable Wepeset.[151]

---

[151] Inconnu-Bocquillon, Danielle, *Le mythe de la déesse lointaine à Philae, BdE 132*, (Le Caire/Cairo: IFAO, 2001), 22.

HYMN OF TEFNUT

Tefnut, Daughter of Ra
Uraeus on His forehead
Eye of Ra, Lady of Senmet
✝The beauty on the Head of Her Father
With the Beautiful Face, Sweet of Love
Mother, Who Gives Birth to the Gods.[152]

---

[152] Inconnu-Bocquillon, Danielle, *Le mythe de la déesse lointaine à Philae, BdE 132,* (Le Caire/Cairo: IFAO, 2001), 23.

Hymn of Tefnut

Tefnut, Daughter of Ra
Wepeset
Lady of Flame in the Castle of Flame
One who consumes Apep with the burning breath of Her mouth
Venerable Wife of Her brother Shu
Who does not stray from Him to any other place.[153]

---

[153] Inconnu-Bocquillon, Danielle, *Le mythe de la déesse lointaine à Philae, BdE 132,* (Le Caire/Cairo: IFAO, 2001), 39.

HYMN OF TEFNUT

Tefnut, Daughter of Ra
Mistress of the Human Race
Regent
Venerable
Coiled One on the Head of Her Father
One Who consumes the enemies
With the burning breath of Her mouth.[154]

---

[154] Inconnu-Bocquillon, Danielle, *Le mythe de la déesse lointaine à Philae, BdE 132*, (Le Caire/Cairo: IFAO, 2001), 43.

HYMN OF TEFNUT

Tefnut, Daughter of Ra
Who resides in the Abaton
August and Perfect
Regent of Philae
One who comes from Kenset to Senmet
And takes Her seat.[155]

---

[155] Inconnu-Bocquillon, Danielle, *Le mythe de la déesse lointaine à Philae, BdE 132*, (Le Caire/Cairo: IFAO, 2001), 45.

HYMN OF TEFNUT

Tefnut, Daughter of Ra
Who resides in Senmet
Great of Carnage on the Place of Execution
Who flies against the enemies of Her son
One who dismembers Her enemies
Queen of Upper and Lower Egypt
Female *Ba* greater than the Gods
Higher than the Goddesses
Mistress of Battle
Lioness
Mistress of Skinning
Superior of the Place of Execution in Eastern Behdet
One who devours relative to Her height.[156]

---

[156] Inconnu-Bocquillon, Danielle, *Le mythe de la déesse lointaine à Philae*, BdE 132, (Le Caire/Cairo: IFAO, 2001), 50.

HYMN OF TEFNUT

Tefnut, Daughter of Ra
Lady of Senmet
Great Flame in the Castle of Flame
Eye of Ra, Mistress of Heaven
Regent of All the Gods.[157]

---

[157] Inconnu-Bocquillon, Danielle, *Le mythe de la déesse lointaine à Philae*, BdE 132, (Le Caire/Cairo: IFAO, 2001), 51.

HYMN OF TEFNUT

Tefnut, Daughter of Ra
Who resides in the Abaton
One who consumes Apep
the enemy of Her Father Ra
Whose heart rejoices when He sees Her
Tefnut, Daughter of Ra
Who resides in the Abaton
Wepeset
Lady of Flame in the Castle of Flame
Tefnut, Daughter of Ra
Lady of the Abaton
Great Flame surrounding Him
One who is stable in Elephantine
One who appears in Senmet.[158]

---

[158] Inconnu-Bocquillon, Danielle, *Le mythe de la déesse lointaine à Philae, BdE 132*, (Le Caire/Cairo: IFAO, 2001), 57.

HYMN OF TEFNUT

Tefnut, Daughter of Ra
Who resides in the Abaton
August and Powerful
Regent of Philae
One from Kenset
In the company of Her brother.[159]

.

---

[159] Inconnu-Bocquillon, Danielle, *Le mythe de la déesse lointaine à Philae, BdE 132*, (Le Caire/Cairo: IFAO, 2001), 61.

HYMN OF TEFNUT

Tefnut, Daughter of Ra
Lady of the Abaton
Great Flame surrounding Him
Flame Who shoots out
Stable in Elephantine
Appearing in Senmet
Queen of Upper and Lower Egypt
Daughter of Ra, whom Her heart loves
One from Ta-Sety
This is the seat where Wepeset stands
While She is angry
When She comes from Bugem.[160]

---

[160] Inconnu-Bocquillon, Danielle, *Le mythe de la déesse lointaine à Philae, BdE 132*, (Le Caire/Cairo: IFAO, 2001), 78.

HYMN OF TEFNUT

Tefnut, Uraeus
Daughter of Ra
At the Head of the House of Flame
Lady of Flame
Who ignites the Two Hills
With the burning breath from Her mouth.[161]

---

[161] Inconnu-Bocquillon, Danielle, *Le mythe de la déesse lointaine à Philae*, BdE 132, (Le Caire/Cairo: IFAO, 2001), 80.

HYMN OF TEFNUT

Tefnut, Daughter of Ra in Senmet
Venerable
Uraeus of Heruakhety
Flame
Powerful, Regent of the Spirits and Emissaries
One who consumes the enemies
with the burning breath of Her mouth
At this place
Her majesty returns to the land of the Pure Place
One who burns Apep with Her flame
As long as Sekhmet is Powerful in Senmet
Burning enemies with Her burning breath
She will burst like flame to the sky
Then Her name will be Sopdet.[162]

---

[162] Inconnu-Bocquillon, Danielle, *Le mythe de la déesse lointaine à Philae, BdE 132*, (Le Caire/Cairo: IFAO, 2001), 83.

HYMN OF TEFNUT

Tefnut, Daughter of Ra
Who resides in the Abaton
Eye of Ra, Mistress of Heaven
Who is at the Head of Philae
August and Powerful
Regent of All the Gods
Flame, Who burns Her enemies
Who is appeased by the glorification of the Two Sistra
As long as the August and Venerable One
Is the One Who appears in Philae
As Mistress of the Red Cloth, Who Loves Brightness
To receive the *Seshesh*-Sistrum and the *Sekhem*-Sistrum
In gold, so that Her heart is appeased by their sight
She is the Lady of Flame
Who burns Her Father's enemies
Tefnut, Daughter of Ra
Who resides in the Abaton.[163]

---

[163] Inconnu-Bocquillon, Danielle, *Le mythe de la déesse lointaine à Philae, BdE 132*, (Le Caire/Cairo: IFAO, 2001), 86.

HYMN OF TEFNUT

Queen of Upper and Lower Egypt
August and Powerful
Eye of Ra
Venerable
Coiled One on the Head of Her Father
One who shoots Apep with Her burning breath
in the morning boat
Tefnut, Daughter of Ra
Who resides in the Abaton.[164]

---

[164] Inconnu-Bocquillon, Danielle, *Le mythe de la déesse lointaine à Philae*, BdE *132*, (Le Caire/Cairo: IFAO, 2001), 87.

HYMN OF TEFNUT

Tefnut, Daughter of Ra
Who resides in the Abaton
Regent and Lady of Philae
Uraeus
Her Father rejoices to see Her
Tefnut, Daughter of Ra
Who resides in the Abaton
Eye of Ra, Mistress of Heaven
Who is at the Head of Philae
August and Venerable
Regent of All the Gods
Flame
Who burns Her enemies
One who is appeased by the Two Lights
As long as the August and Venerable is the Perfect One
Daughter of Ra, Who Loves Her
To receive the *wensheb* from the arms of Ra's son
To rejoice in Her heart to see Her
She is the Eye of Ra
Who illuminates the Two Lands
Tefnut
One who resides in the Castle of the Front.[165]

---

[165] Inconnu-Bocquillon, Danielle, *Le mythe de la déesse lointaine à Philae, BdE 132*, (Le Caire/Cairo: IFAO, 2001), 88.

HYMN OF TEFNUT

Tefnut, Daughter of Ra
Who resides in the Abaton
Regent of the Goddesses
Queen of Upper and Lower Egypt
Daughter of Ra, Whom Her Heart Loves
One from Ta-Sety
Her seat is where Wepeset stands
While She is angry
When She comes from Bugem.[166]

---

[166] Inconnu-Bocquillon, Danielle, *Le mythe de la déesse lointaine à Philae, BdE 132*, (Le Caire/Cairo: IFAO, 2001), 92.

HYMN OF TEFNUT

Tefnut, Daughter of Ra
Who resides in the Abaton
One who burns the enemies of Her Father Ra
Who protects His majesty daily
And unites with Him in Senmet.[167]

---

[167] Inconnu-Bocquillon, Danielle, *Le mythe de la déesse lointaine à Philae, BdE 132*, (Le Caire/Cairo: IFAO, 2001), 93.

HYMN OF TEFNUT

Tefnut, Daughter of Ra
Who resides in the Abaton
August and Powerful
Regent of Philae
One who comes from Kenset to Egypt
And makes Her seat in Senmet
In the company of Her brother.[168]

---

[168] Inconnu-Bocquillon, Danielle, *Le mythe de la déesse lointaine à Philae, BdE 132*, (Le Caire/Cairo: IFAO, 2001), 97.

HYMN OF TEFNUT

Tefnut, Daughter of Ra
Uraeus of Ra, Lady of the Abaton
Regent and Lady of Philae
Mistress of the Sky
Regent of All the Gods.[169]

---

[169] Inconnu-Bocquillon, Danielle, *Le mythe de la déesse lointaine à Philae, BdE 132,* (Le Caire/Cairo: IFAO, 2001), 101.

HYMN OF TEFNUT

Tefnut, Daughter of Ra
Who resides in the Abaton
August and Powerful
One Who springs from Kenset
Tefnut, Daughter of Ra
Who resides in the Abaton
August and Powerful
One Who springs from Kenset
Coming toward Senmet
In the form of Wepeset
Tefnut, Daughter of Ra
Lady of Senmet
Regent and Lady of Philae.[170]

---

[170] Inconnu-Bocquillon, Danielle, *Le mythe de la déesse lointaine à Philae, BdE 132*, (Le Caire/Cairo: IFAO, 2001), 109.

Hymn of Tefnut

Tefnut, Daughter of Ra
Who resides in the Abaton
Tefnut, Daughter of Ra
Who resides in the Abaton
Wepeset, Venerable, Lady of Senmet
Tefnut, Daughter of Ra
Who resides in the Abaton
Wepeset, Venerable, Lady of Senmet.[171]

[171] Inconnu-Bocquillon, Danielle, *Le mythe de la déesse lointaine à Philae*, BdE 132, (Le Caire/Cairo: IFAO, 2001), 113.

HYMN OF TEFNUT

Tefnut, Daughter of Ra
Who resides in the Abaton
Venerable, *Uraeus*
Lady of Senmet
Eye of Ra, Mistress of the Sky
Regent of All the Gods.[172]

---

[172] Inconnu-Bocquillon, Danielle, *Le mythe de la déesse lointaine à Philae, BdE 132*, (Le Caire/Cairo: IFAO, 2001), 114.

HYMN OF TEFNUT

Tefnut, Daughter of Ra
Who resides in the Abaton
August and Perfect
Lady of Philae
Sovereign in Senmet
Tefnut, Daughter of Ra
Who resides in the Abaton
August and Perfect
Lady of Philae
Sovereign in Senmet
Tefnut, Daughter of Ra
Who resides in the Abaton.[173]

---

[173] Inconnu-Bocquillon, Danielle, *Le mythe de la déesse lointaine à Philae*, BdE 132, (Le Caire/Cairo: IFAO, 2001), 117.

HYMN OF TEFNUT

Tefnut, Daughter of Ra in Philae
Great Flame Goddess in Senmet.[174]

---

[174] Kockelmann, Holger and Erich Winter, *Philae III: Die Zweite Ostkolonnade des Tempels der Isis in Philae. (CO II und CO II K)*, (Verlag der Osterreichischen Akademie der Wissenschaften/Austrian Academy of Sciences, 2016), 141.

HYMN OF TEFNUT

Tefnut, Daughter of Ra, Lady of the Abaton
In whose vicinity is the Great Flame
One Who Burns with Fire, Dwelling in Elephantine
And appears in Senmet for all eternity.[175]

---

[175] Kockelmann, Holger and Erich Winter, *Philae III: Die Zweite Ostkolonnade des Tempels der Isis in Philae. (CO II und CO II K)*, (Verlag der Osterreichischen Akademie der Wissenschaften/Austrian Academy of Sciences, 2016), 189.

HYMN OF TEFNUT

Tefnut
Daughter of Ra on the Abaton
Great Flame Goddess.[176]

---

[176] Kockelmann, Holger and Erich Winter, *Philae III: Die Zweite Ostkolonnade des Tempels der Isis in Philae. (CO II und CO II K)*, (Verlag der Osterreichischen Akademie der Wissenschaften/Austrian Academy of Sciences, 2016), 231.

HYMN OF TEFNUT

Tefnut
Uraeus Snake
Princess of Life, the House of Birth
She cleans Her city for Her son Heru.[177]

---

[177] Kockelmann, Holger and Erich Winter, *Philae III: Die Zweite Ostkolonnade des Tempels der Isis in Philae. (CO II und CO II K)*, (Verlag der Osterreichischen Akademie der Wissenschaften/Austrian Academy of Sciences, 2016), 263.

HYMN OF TEFNUT

Tefnut, Daughter of Ra
In the midst of the Abaton
Eye of Ra
Uraeus on His Forehead.[178]

---

[178] Kockelmann, Holger and Erich Winter, *Philae III: Die Zweite Ostkolonnade des Tempels der Isis in Philae. (CO II und CO II K)*, (Verlag der Osterreichischen Akademie der Wissenschaften/Austrian Academy of Sciences, 2016), 292.

HYMN OF TEFNUT

Tefnut, Daughter of Ra
Who resides in Biggeh, Mistress of the Gods.[179]

---

[179] Gaber, Amr. "The Central Hall in the Egyptian Temples of the Ptolemaic Period." (PhD diss., Durham University, 2009), 363.

HYMN OF TEFNUT

Tefnut, Daughter of Ra
Who resides in Abaton, Who puts your victory against your
enemies.[180]

---

[180] Gaber, Amr. "The Central Hall in the Egyptian Temples of the Ptolemaic Period."
(PhD diss., Durham University, 2009), 402.

Excerpt Hymn of Tefnut

Tefnut in Senmet
Who unites with Her brother
Who Causes *Bau* to Flourish (Shu),
In the Abaton.[181]

---

[181] Inconnu-Bocquillon, Danielle, *Le mythe de la déesse lointaine à Philae, BdE 132*, (Le Caire/Cairo: IFAO, 2001), 119. Thank you to Rev. Dr. Tamara L. Siuda for her help with this translation.

TEMPLE OF OPET

HYMN OF TEFNUT

Tefnut, Daughter of Ra
Sovereign of the Gods
Uraeus in Her moment of fury
Who protected...assemble
Amun said in relation to Her
That Her flame came out of the Goddesses
And so She became a flame like what came out of Her mouth
In order to overthrow the enemies of Onnophris.[182]

---

[182] De Wit, Constant. *Les Inscriptions du Temple d'Opet a Karnak III: Traduction integrale des textes rituels-Essai d'interpretation.* (Bruxelles : Edition de la Fondation Egyptologique Reine Elisabeth, 1968), 52.

HYMN OF TEFNUT

Tefnut, Daughter of Ra
Mother of God
Who Gave Birth to the Gods
Eye of Ra
Lady of Heaven
Sovereign of All the Gods.[183]

---

[183] De Wit, Constant. *Les Inscriptions du Temple d'Opet a Karnak III: Traduction integrale des textes rituels-Essai d'interpretation*. (Bruxelles : Edition de la Fondation Egyptologique Reine Elisabeth, 1968), 89.

TEMPLE OF KOM OMBO

HYMN OF TEFNUT

I enter Egypt with My brother
We do not go away from you
We slaughter your enemies
I send the flame against the enemy of the son of Ra.[184]

---

[184] Gutbub, Adolphe. *Textes fondamentaux de la théologie de Kom Ombo.* (Institut français d'archéologie orientale du Caire, 1973), 380.

HYMN TO TEFNUT

It is the Place of Joy
The Young Birds of Ra
They rejoice in it
It is the House of Joy
Image of Atum
Castle of Jubilation of Tefnut, the Great
They unite there, they meet in peace
They join gently in heart
Their heir is by their side
United with Them as the Ancestor-Nourisher
Father of the Gods
While He turns into a young man
Living from birth
Lord of Ailments
Who gives to the one He loves.[185]

---

[185] Gutbub, Adolphe. *Textes fondamentaux de la théologie de Kom Ombo.* (Institut français d'archéologie orientale du Caire, 1973), 186.

HYMN TO TEFNUT

This beautiful House is the residence of Shu
It is the Throne of Geb
The beautiful platform of Tefnut, Daughter of Ra
Beautiful to See (Belvedere) of the Gods and Goddesses
Protective staircase of the protective Gods
Block to slaughter the enemies
City of where sustainable offerings are presented
House where life is raised
Lasting until eternity
With the majesty of Heru Wer and Sobek, Lord of Ombos.[186]

---

[186] Gutbub, Adolphe. *Textes fondamentaux de la théologie de Kom Ombo.* (Institut français d'archéologie orientale du Caire, 1973), 312.

INSCRIPTION OF TEFNUT

Tefnut, with Her daughter Nut.[187]

---

[187] Gutbub, Adolphe. *Textes fondamentaux de la théologie de Kom Ombo*. (Institut français d'archéologie orientale du Caire, 1973), 2.

INSCRIPTION OF TEFNUT

Tefnut, as the Good Sister (*Tasenetnofret*), Aset.
She is there under the name of Hethert
Who pours fresh water for Her father Ra.[188]

---

[188] Gutbub, Adolphe. *Textes fondamentaux de la théologie de Kom Ombo*. (Institut français d'archéologie orientale du Caire, 1973), 3.

HYMNS FROM *DER AUSZUG DER HATHOR-TEFNUT AUS NUBIEN*

HYMN OF TEFNUT

Tefnut, Mistress of Women.[189]

---

[189] Junker, Hermann. "Der Auszug der Hathor-Tefnut aus Nubien." *Abhandlungen der Preußischen Akademie der Wissenschaften, philosophisch-historische Klasse* (1911), 82.

HYMN OF TEFNUT

Tefnut, Mistress of Bugem.[190]

𓏏

---

[190] Junker, Hermann. "Der Auszug der Hathor-Tefnut aus Nubien." *Abhandlungen der Preußischen Akademie der Wissenschaften, philosophisch-historische Klasse* (1911), 82.

HYMN OF TEFNUT

House of Shu and House of Tefnut.
House, Who Loves Tefnut
Place of which Djehuty said:
One is happy here.[191]

---

[191] Junker, Hermann. "Der Auszug der Hathor-Tefnut aus Nubien." *Abhandlungen der Preußischen Akademie der Wissenschaften, philosophisch-historische Klasse* (1911), 83.

HYMN OF TEFNUT

Tefnut, the Great
The Good *rpj.t*
That came from Bugem.[192]

---

[192] Junker, Hermann. "Der Auszug der Hathor-Tefnut aus Nubien." *Abhandlungen der Preußischen Akademie der Wissenschaften, philosophisch-historische Klasse* (1911), 83.

HYMN OF TEFNUT

Mehyt, Tefnut in Edfu
The sacred obelisk
She protects with Her brother.
Hethert, Mistress of Dendera
Tefnut in Edfu
Who embraced Shu in the Leg Chamber.[193]

---

[193] Junker, Hermann. "Der Auszug der Hathor-Tefnut aus Nubien." *Abhandlungen der Preußischen Akademie der Wissenschaften, philosophisch-historische Klasse* (1911), 22.

HYMN OF TEFNUT

Tefnut, Daughter of Ra
On the Abaton
Splendid, Beautiful
Mistress of Philae.[194]

---

[194] Junker, Hermann. "Der Auszug der Hathor-Tefnut aus Nubien." *Abhandlungen der Preußischen Akademie der Wissenschaften, philosophisch-historische Klasse* (1911), 32.

HYMN OF TEFNUT

Tefnut, Who is from Nubia
After the Eye of Ra came
Who took place in Senmet with Her brother Shu.[195]

---

[195] Junker, Hermann. "Der Auszug der Hathor-Tefnut aus Nubien." *Abhandlungen der Preußischen Akademie der Wissenschaften, philosophisch-historische Klasse* (1911), 33.

HYMN OF TEFNUT

Tefnut, Daughter of Ra
On the Abaton
Who came from Bugem with Her brother Shu.[196]

---

[196] Junker, Hermann. "Der Auszug der Hathor-Tefnut aus Nubien." *Abhandlungen der Preußischen Akademie der Wissenschaften, philosophisch-historische Klasse* (1911), 33.

HYMN OF TEFNUT

Tefnut, as Hethert the Great
Lady of Senmet, therein.
At Her (Aset) side.
They repel the evil
From the place
Where the Majesty of Wesir is.[197]

---

[197] Junker, Hermann. "Der Auszug der Hathor-Tefnut aus Nubien." *Abhandlungen der Preußischen Akademie der Wissenschaften, philosophisch-historische Klasse* (1911), 35.

HYMN OF TEFNUT

Tefnut, Mistress of Senmet
Princess
Mistress of Philae.[198]

---

[198] Junker, Hermann. "Der Auszug der Hathor-Tefnut aus Nubien." *Abhandlungen der Preußischen Akademie der Wissenschaften, philosophisch-historische Klasse* (1911), 52.

HYMN OF TEFNUT

Tefnut, Daughter of Ra on the Abaton
Great Flame Goddess in Senmet.[199]

---

[199] Junker, Hermann. "Der Auszug der Hathor-Tefnut aus Nubien." *Abhandlungen der Preußischen Akademie der Wissenschaften, philosophisch-historische Klasse* (1911), 52.

HYMN OF TEFNUT

Tefnut, Mistress of Philae
Who came from the Nubian country.[200]

---

[200] Junker, Hermann. "Der Auszug der Hathor-Tefnut aus Nubien." *Abhandlungen der Preußischen Akademie der Wissenschaften, philosophisch-historische Klasse* (1911), 52.

HYMN OF TEFNUT

Tefnut, Daughter of Ra on the Abaton
Venerable, Powerful One
Came from Kenset.[201]

---

[201] Junker, Hermann. "Der Auszug der Hathor-Tefnut aus Nubien." *Abhandlungen der Preußischen Akademie der Wissenschaften, philosophisch-historische Klasse* (1911), 53.

HYMN OF TEFNUT

Tefnut, With a Red Face
against Her son's enemy
Destroying his adversary.[202]

[202] Junker, Hermann. "Der Auszug der Hathor-Tefnut aus Nubien." *Abhandlungen der Preußischen Akademie der Wissenschaften, philosophisch-historische Klasse* (1911), 36.

HYMN OF TEFNUT

Tefnut, Daughter of Ra on the Abaton
Great Wepeset
Mistress of Senmet.[203]

---

[203] Junker, Hermann. "Der Auszug der Hathor-Tefnut aus Nubien." *Abhandlungen der Preußischen Akademie der Wissenschaften, philosophisch-historische Klasse* (1911), 55.

HYMN OF TEFNUT

Tefnut, Daughter of Ra on the Abaton
Great Wepeset, Mistress of Senmet.[204]

---

[204] Junker, Hermann. "Der Auszug der Hathor-Tefnut aus Nubien." *Abhandlungen der Preußischen Akademie der Wissenschaften, philosophisch-historische Klasse* (1911), 55.

HYMN OF TEFNUT-TASENETNOFRET

Tasenetnofret, Tefnut
On the Great Seat.[205]

---

[205] Junker, Hermann. "Der Auszug der Hathor-Tefnut aus Nubien." *Abhandlungen der Preußischen Akademie der Wissenschaften, philosophisch-historische Klasse* (1911), 61.

HYMN OF TEFNUT-TASENETNOFRET

Tasenetnofret, Mistress of Ombos
Tefnut, Diadem of Her Father Ra.[206]

---

[206] Junker, Hermann. "Der Auszug der Hathor-Tefnut aus Nubien." *Abhandlungen der Preußischen Akademie der Wissenschaften, philosophisch-historische Klasse* (1911), 61.

HYMN OF TEFNUT-TASENETNOFRET

Tasenetnofret, Tefnut
Daughter of Ra in Ombos.[207]

---

[207] Junker, Hermann. "Der Auszug der Hathor-Tefnut aus Nubien." *Abhandlungen der Preußischen Akademie der Wissenschaften, philosophisch-historische Klasse* (1911), 61.

HYMN OF TEFNUT-TASENETNOFRET

Good Sister
Tefnut
Mistress of Ombos
Mistress of Drunkenness
Who Created Everything
You come
You come in peace to Your city.[208]

Egypt in peace came to this seat
With Her brother Shu
Djehuty appeased Her majesty.[209]

---

[208] Junker, Hermann. "Der Auszug der Hathor-Tefnut aus Nubien." *Abhandlungen der Preußischen Akademie der Wissenschaften, philosophisch-historische Klasse* (1911), 61.
[209] Junker, Hermann. "Der Auszug der Hathor-Tefnut aus Nubien." *Abhandlungen der Preußischen Akademie der Wissenschaften, philosophisch-historische Klasse* (1911), 61.

HYMN OF TEFNUT-TASENETNOFRET

Tefnut, the Good Sister
Mistress of Ombos
Great Flame Goddess
with Her brother.[210]

---

[210] Junker, Hermann. "Der Auszug der Hathor-Tefnut aus Nubien." *Abhandlungen der Preußischen Akademie der Wissenschaften, philosophisch-historische Klasse* (1911), 62.

HYMN OF TEFNUT

Tefnut, Daughter of Ra
Mistress of Ombos
Eye of Ra, Mistress of Heaven
Her majesty came from Kenset
And settled with Her brother, Shu
In this town.[211]

---

[211] Junker, Hermann. "Der Auszug der Hathor-Tefnut aus Nubien." *Abhandlungen der Preußischen Akademie der Wissenschaften, philosophisch-historische Klasse* (1911), 62.

Hymn of Tefnut

The Good Sister, Tefnut
Mistress of Ombos
Ruler of the Gods and Goddesses
Splendid, h3t
Whose sight is so beautiful
Eye of Ra encircling the sun
Splendid
Good Wife of Her brother Shu
Splendid
She came from Kenset with Him
They united in Their city in joy.[212]

[212] Junker, Hermann. "Der Auszug der Hathor-Tefnut aus Nubien." *Abhandlungen der Preußischen Akademie der Wissenschaften, philosophisch-historische Klasse* (1911), 65.

HYMN OF TEFNUT-TASENETNOFRET

The Good Sister, Tefnut
Mistress of Ombos
Eye of Ra, who came from Kenset.[213]

---

[213] Junker, Hermann. "Der Auszug der Hathor-Tefnut aus Nubien." *Abhandlungen der Preußischen Akademie der Wissenschaften, philosophisch-historische Klasse* (1911), 68.

HYMN OF TEFNUT

Tefnut, the Great
Shu performed the dances
He danced in jubilation in front of Her
when She came to Her town
at the *ub.t wur.*
Her brother is dancing in front of Her.
The Living Image of Shu in Esna
Who dances for the Lioness Goddess
Nebetuu
Who makes His Mistress happy
With what She loves.[214]

---

[214] Junker, Hermann. "Der Auszug der Hathor-Tefnut aus Nubien." *Abhandlungen der Preußischen Akademie der Wissenschaften, philosophisch-historische Klasse* (1911), 71-72.

HYMN OF TEFNUT

Tefnut, Daughter of Ra in Dendera
Sekhmet, the Mighty One
Mistress of Demons
Flame Goddess, Mighty One
Hethert, the Great
Mistress of Dendera.[215]

---

[215] Junker, Hermann. "Der Auszug der Hathor-Tefnut aus Nubien." *Abhandlungen der Preußischen Akademie der Wissenschaften, philosophisch-historische Klasse* (1911), 84-85.

OTHER HYMNS

HYMN OF TEFNUT

Tefnut, Daughter of Ra
Mistress of All the Gods
Divine Mother
Who resides in Iatdi
Whose flame is great against Set
Who reaches the members of Her opponents
Who slaughters the enemies of the House of the Sistrum.[216]

---

[216] Preys, René. *Les complexes de la Demeure du Sistre et du Trône de Rê: théologie et décoration dans le temple d'Hathor à Dendera.* Vol. 106. (Peeters Publishers, 2002), 205.

HYMN OF TEFNUT

With the Head of Lapis
Female Disk
Lady of the Disk in Iatdi
Tefnut
Daughter of Ra
Mistress of the Goddesses.[217]

---

[217] Husson, Constance. L'offrande du miroir dans les temples égyptiens de l'époque gréco-romaine. (France: Audin, 1977), 159.

HYMN OF TEFNUT

Tefnut, Daughter of Ra
Who resides in the Abaton
Great *Uraeus*, Lady of Senmet
Eye of Ra, Lady of the Sky
Mistress of All the Gods.[218]

---

[218] Preys, René. "Le mythe de la Lointaine: Lionne dangereuse et déesse bénéfique." In *Sphinx: Les gardiens de l'Egypte*, pp. 145. Fonds Mercator, 2006.

HYMN OF TEFNUT

Tefnut, Daughter of Ra.[219]

---

[219] Preys, René. "Le mythe de la Lointaine: Lionne dangereuse et déesse bénéfique." In *Sphinx: Les gardiens de l'Egypte*, pp. 146. Fonds Mercator, 2006.

HYMN OF TEFNUT

Tefnut, the Daughter of Ra
One who comes from Nubia.[220]

---

[220] Preys, René. "Le mythe de la Lointaine: Lionne dangereuse et déesse bénéfique." In *Sphinx: Les gardiens de l'Egypte*, pp. 146. Fonds Mercator, 2006.

HYMN OF TEFNUT

Tefnut, Daughter of Ra
Who resides in the Abaton.[221]

---

[221] Preys, René. "Le mythe de la Lointaine: Lionne dangereuse et déesse bénéfique." In *Sphinx: Les gardiens de l'Egypte*, pp. 146. Fonds Mercator, 2006.

HYMN OF TEFNUT

Venerable, Powerful
One who comes out of Kenset
Who is heading to Biggeh as Wepeset.[222]

---

[222] Preys, René. "Le mythe de la Lointaine: Lionne dangereuse et déesse bénéfique." In *Sphinx: Les gardiens de l'Egypte*, pp. 146. Fonds Mercator, 2006.

HYMN OF TEFNUT

Tefnut, Daughter of Ra
Mistress of the Goddesses.[223]

---

[223] Husson, Constance. L'offrande du miroir dans les temples égyptiens de l'époque gréco-romaine. (France: Audin, 1977), 159.

Hymn of Tefnut

Tefnut, Daughter of Ra, Hair of Edfu
August, Powerful in Iatdi.[224]

---

[224] Aufrère, Sydney. *L'univers minéral dans la pensée égyptienne*. Vol. 1. (Imp. de l'Institut
français d'archéologie orientale, 1991), 244.

HYMN OF TEFNUT

Tefnut, Daughter of Ra
Eye of Ra in Iatdi.[225]

---

[225] Aufrère, Sydney. *L'univers minéral dans la pensée égyptienne.* Vol. 1. (Imp. de l'Institut français d'archéologie orientale, 1991), 244.

HYMN OF TEFNUT

Tefnut, Daughter of Ra
In the House of Flame
Lady of Flame
Who sets fire to the Two Cliffs
By means of the flame from Her mouth.[226]

---

[226] Aufrère, Sydney. *L'univers minéral dans la pensée égyptienne.* Vol. 1. (Imp. de l'Institut français d'archéologie orientale, 1991), 244.

HYMN OF TEFNUT

Tefnut, Daughter of Ra
Mistress of Xois
Eye of Ra
Mistress of Heaven
Sovereign of All the Gods.[227]

---

[227] Guermeur, Ivan and Christophe Thiers. "Un éloge xoïte de Ptolémée Philadelphe. La stèle BM EA 616". *Bulletin de l'Institut français d'archéologie orientale*, IFAO, 2001), pp.199.

HYMN OF TEFNUT-TASENETNOFRET

Tasenetnofret, Tefnut
Mistress of Ombos
Eye of the Sun
Mistress of the Sky
Regent of All the Gods
Diadem on His Forehead.[228]

---

[228] Piehl, Karl. <u>Inscriptions hiéroglyphiques recueillies en Égypte</u>. (Germany: n.p., 1890), 96.

HYMN OF TEFNUT-TASENETNOFRET

Tefnut, Daughter of the Sun
Mistress of Ombos
Tasenetnofret
Who lives in the Palace of the Hawk
She Who Places Her Brother on the Throne
When She returns from Asia.[229]

[229] Piehl, Karl. Inscriptions hiéroglyphiques recueillies en Égypte. (Germany: n.p., 1890), 99.

HYMN OF TEFNUT

Tefnut, Fire
Destroying Her opponents
as She does in the necropolis
She is like the *Menit*
Eye of the Sun
Whose pupil is frightful
Powerful Seshat
Mistress of All the Goddesses of that name.[230]

---

[230] Piehl, Karl. Inscriptions hiéroglyphiques recueillies en Égypte. (Germany: n.p., 1890), 64.

HYMN OF TEFNUT (LEIDEN MAGICAL PAPYRUS 12)

Ethiopian Cat
Daughter of Ra
Mistress of the Uraeus.[231]

---

[231] Spiegelberg, Wilhelm. *Der ägyptische Mythus vom Sonnenauge*. (Georg Olms Verlag, 1917), 2.

AWAKEN HYMN TO SHU AND TEFNUT

Shu and Tefnut,
Awaken in Peace!
Awaken Peacefully!
May the Two Birds of Ra,
Awaken in Peace!
Awaken Peacefully!
May the Two Children of Atum,
Awaken in Peace!
Awaken Peacefully!
Awake, the Two Children as Eyes
In Peace, Awaken Peacefully!
Let the Lion and Lioness, Awaken!
Ancestor Gods,
Son of Tatenen, Born of Ra,
Atum and His Two Birds,
Flood together with the Grassland,
In their names of Khnum and Nebetuu,
the Great Gods who are Your Ka,
United with Your bodies,
Let the Mother of God awaken,
Peaceful with You
And She does not depart from You,
Ever![232]

---

[232] Sauneron, Serge, *Esna V: Les fêtes religieuses d'Esna aux derniers siècles du paganisme,* (Cairo: IFAO, 1962; 2004), 90. Excerpt from a hymn. Translated by Chelsea Bolton.

Figure 4: The Goddess Tefnut as lioness from the Temple of Dakka.
Photo taken by Roland Unger.
Permission to use under GNU License.
Link: https://en.wikipedia.org/wiki/GNU_Free_Documentation_License

THE TWIN LIONS

Festival Calendar of Tefnut and Shu

This festival calendar has processions, feasts and festivals. There are also *Chronokrater* days or days that are sacred to each god. The New Year festival for this calendar starts in August, but this is a personal preference. The calendar can be calculated from the New Year date which for modern practitioners can be from July thru September. For this calendar, the dates are the ancient Egyptian ones so the 9th day of the month 1st Akhet/Thoth is a Tefnut *Chronokrater* day.

Anhur/Onuris (Bringer of the Distant One) is a praise-name of Shu. The Distant One or Wandering Goddess refers to Tefnut.[233]

Tasenentnofret (Tasenetneferet) means (The Good/Beautiful Sister) and is a praise-name and form of Tefnut or Hethert at the Temple of Kom Ombo. Tasenetnofret listed in this calendar can be any of these three goddesses (Tefnut, or Hethert, or Tasenetnofret Herself). Since it is unclear (in most cases) which goddess the name is referring to, all festivals for Tasenetnofret are listed below. Since this is a calendar for Tefnut, anyone can honor Tefnut in Her name of Tasenetnofret on these holidays.

Monthly Festivals

3rd and 4th Day of Lunar Month: Sacred to Shu and Tefnut[234]
3rd Day of Lunar Month (Chronokrater): Shu[235]
4th Day of Lunar Month (Chronokrater): Tefnut[236]

---

[233] Siuda, Tamara L. The Ancient Egyptian Daybook. (Stargazer Design, 2016), 140.
[234] Leitz, Christian, and Dagmar Budde, et. al. Lexikon der Ägyptischen Götter und Götterbezeichnungen (LGG, OLA 116, Band 7). (Peeters, 2002), 36-37.
[235] Siuda, Tamara L. The Ancient Egyptian Daybook. (Stargazer Design, 2016), 304.
[236] Siuda, Tamara L. The Ancient Egyptian Daybook. (Stargazer Design, 2016), 304.

Yearly Festivals

1st Akhet/Thoth/August

1—New Year (*Wep Ronpet*); Appearance of Tasenetnofret[237]

2—Feast of Shu, Son of Ra[238]

2—Feast of Onuris (Shu) of Heliopolis[239]

2—Chronokrater: Shu[240]

9—Chronokrater: Tefnut[241]

10—Chronokrater: Tefnut; Feast of Tefnut-Nebtu[242]

10—Feast of Tefnut; Feast of Tefnut in Iunet (Dendera)[243]

17—Chronokrater: Tefnut and Tefnut, Who Gave Birth to Her Father[244]

18 thru 22—Feast of Shu and Tefnut (5 Days)[245]

18 thru 22 –Procession of the Goddess Tefnut and Her Ennead (5 Days)[246]

18 thru 22—Drunkenness Festival: Tefnut-Hethert Returns to Egypt[247]

19—Festival of Heru-Shu, Son of Ra[248]

19—Festival of Shu and Hethert-Tefnut[249]

25—Chronokater: Tefnut, Consort of the Gods[250]

2nd Akhet/Paopi/September

1—Day When Shu and Tefnut Go Out to Judge the Followers of His Majesty[251]

3—Appearance of Tasenetnofret[252]

---

[237] Siuda, Tamara L. The Ancient Egyptian Daybook. (Stargazer Design, 2016), 46.

[238] Siuda, Tamara L. The Ancient Egyptian Daybook. (Stargazer Design, 2016), 48.

[239] Siuda, Tamara L. The Ancient Egyptian Daybook. (Stargazer Design, 2016), 48.

[240] Siuda, Tamara L. The Ancient Egyptian Daybook. (Stargazer Design, 2016), 48.

[241] Siuda, Tamara L. The Ancient Egyptian Daybook. (Stargazer Design, 2016), 53.

[242] Siuda, Tamara L. The Ancient Egyptian Daybook. (Stargazer Design, 2016), 54.

[243] Lafont, Julie. "Consommation et proscription du miel en Égypte ancienne. Quand bj.t devient bw.t," in BIFAO 116 (2016), p. 102.

[244] Siuda, Tamara L. The Ancient Egyptian Daybook. (Stargazer Design, 2016), 59.

[245] Siuda, Tamara L. The Ancient Egyptian Daybook. (Stargazer Design, 2016), 59-65.

[246] Siuda, Tamara L. The Ancient Egyptian Daybook. (Stargazer Design, 2016), 63-66.

[247] Siuda, Tamara L. The Ancient Egyptian Daybook. (Stargazer Design, 2016), 59-60.

[248] Siuda, Tamara L. The Ancient Egyptian Daybook. (Stargazer Design, 2016), 62.

[249] Siuda, Tamara L. The Ancient Egyptian Daybook. (Stargazer Design, 2016), 161.

[250] Siuda, Tamara L. The Ancient Egyptian Daybook. (Stargazer Design, 2016), 67.

[251] Siuda, Tamara L. The Ancient Egyptian Daybook. (Stargazer Design, 2016), 75.

7 thru 10–Appearance of Tasenetnofret (4 days)[253]

8–Chronokrater: Tefnut[254]

9–Chronokrater: Tefnut, Daughter of Ra[255]

11–Chronokrater: Tefnut[256]

15–Procession of Tefnut, Daughter of Ra[257]

16–Chronokrater: Tefnut[258]

16–Chronokrater: Onuris[259]

16–Feast of the Eye of Heru, Shu Brings It Back[260]

3rd Akhet/Hethara/October

2–Chronokrater: Onuris[261]

4–Chronokrater: Tefnut[262]

7–Chronokrater: Tefnut, Lady of the Angry Glance or Tefnut, Lady of the Primordial Time[263]

12–Chronokrater: Shu[264]

21–Feast of Shu, Son of Ra[265]

25–Shu, Son of Ra[266]

26–Chronokrater: Onuris[267]

4th Akhet/Koiak/November

1–Procession of Nebtu as Hethert-Tefnut and Her Followers[268]

---

[252] Siuda, Tamara L. The Ancient Egyptian Daybook. (Stargazer Design, 2016), 76-77.

[253] Siuda, Tamara L. The Ancient Egyptian Daybook. (Stargazer Design, 2016), 79-80.

[254] Siuda, Tamara L. The Ancient Egyptian Daybook. (Stargazer Design, 2016), 80.

[255] Siuda, Tamara L. The Ancient Egyptian Daybook. (Stargazer Design, 2016), 81.

[256] Siuda, Tamara L. The Ancient Egyptian Daybook. (Stargazer Design, 2016), 81-82.

[257] Siuda, Tamara L. The Ancient Egyptian Daybook. (Stargazer Design, 2016), 83-84.

[258] Siuda, Tamara L. The Ancient Egyptian Daybook. (Stargazer Design, 2016), 84.

[259] Siuda, Tamara L. The Ancient Egyptian Daybook. (Stargazer Design, 2016), 84.

[260] Siuda, Tamara L. The Ancient Egyptian Daybook. (Stargazer Design, 2016), 84.

[261] Siuda, Tamara L. The Ancient Egyptian Daybook. (Stargazer Design, 2016), 95.

[262] Siuda, Tamara L. The Ancient Egyptian Daybook. (Stargazer Design, 2016), 96.

[263] Siuda, Tamara L. The Ancient Egyptian Daybook. (Stargazer Design, 2016), 97.

[264] Siuda, Tamara L. The Ancient Egyptian Daybook. (Stargazer Design, 2016), 99.

[265] Siuda, Tamara L. The Ancient Egyptian Daybook. (Stargazer Design, 2016), 103.

[266] Siuda, Tamara L. The Ancient Egyptian Daybook. (Stargazer Design, 2016), 105.

[267] Siuda, Tamara L. The Ancient Egyptian Daybook. (Stargazer Design, 2016), 105.

[268] Siuda, Tamara L. The Ancient Egyptian Daybook. (Stargazer Design, 2016), 114-115.

5—Chronokrater: Tefnut, Consort of the Gods[269]
17—Chronokrater: Onuris and Onuris-Shu, Son of Ra[270]
24—Chronokrater: Hethert-Tefnut, Lady of Praise[271]
27—Chronokrater: Tefnut, Daughter of Ra[272]

1 Peret/Tybi/December
1—Feast of Tefnut[273]
6—Appearance of Tasenetnofret[274]
13—Chronokrater: Tefnut[275]
13—Chronokrater: Shu, Lord of Ma'at[276]
14—Chronorkrater: Tefnut[277]
16—Appearance of Heru-Shu[278]
17—Chronokrater: Onuris[279]
1 Peret 19 thru 2 Peret 4: Feast of the Return of the Wandering Eye
  Goddess (Solstice)[280]
21—Feast of Shu[281]
22—Chronokrater: Onuris[282]
29—Chronokrater: Onuris[283]

2 Peret/Mechir/January
5—Chronokrater: Tefnut[284]

[269] Siuda, Tamara L. The Ancient Egyptian Daybook. (Stargazer Design, 2016), 116-117.
[270] Siuda, Tamara L. The Ancient Egyptian Daybook. (Stargazer Design, 2016), 123.
[271] Siuda, Tamara L. The Ancient Egyptian Daybook. (Stargazer Design, 2016), 128.
[272] Siuda, Tamara L. The Ancient Egyptian Daybook. (Stargazer Design, 2016), 132.
[273] Siuda, Tamara L. The Ancient Egyptian Daybook. (Stargazer Design, 2016), 142-143.
[274] Siuda, Tamara L. The Ancient Egyptian Daybook. (Stargazer Design, 2016), 146.
[275] Siuda, Tamara L. The Ancient Egyptian Daybook. (Stargazer Design, 2016), 149.
[276] Siuda, Tamara L. The Ancient Egyptian Daybook. (Stargazer Design, 2016), 149.
[277] Siuda, Tamara L. The Ancient Egyptian Daybook. (Stargazer Design, 2016), 149.
[278] Siuda, Tamara L. The Ancient Egyptian Daybook. (Stargazer Design, 2016), 150-151.
[279] Siuda, Tamara L. The Ancient Egyptian Daybook. (Stargazer Design, 2016), 151.
[280] Siuda, Tamara L. The Ancient Egyptian Daybook. (Stargazer Design, 2016), 140, 152
  and 162.
[281] Siuda, Tamara L. The Ancient Egyptian Daybook. (Stargazer Design, 2016), 154.
[282] Siuda, Tamara L. The Ancient Egyptian Daybook. (Stargazer Design, 2016), 154.
[283] Siuda, Tamara L. The Ancient Egyptian Daybook. (Stargazer Design, 2016), 158.
[284] Siuda, Tamara L. The Ancient Egyptian Daybook. (Stargazer Design, 2016), 164.

6—Feast of Shu[285]

12—Chronokrater: Tefnut[286]

21 thru 22—Feast of Heru-Shu[287]

23—Chronokrater: Tefnut, Lady of Faience[288]

3 Peret/Pamenot/February

15—Chronokrater: Onuris[289]

21—Chronokrater: Onuris[290]

26—Chronokrater: Onuris[291]

27—Chronokrater: Tefnut-Sekhmet, Great in Millions[292]

4 Peret/Parmuthi/March

1—Chronokrater: Tefnut[293]

Day After New Moon—Mystery of the Divine Birth: Tefnut and Her Son[294]

10—Appearance of Tasenetnofret[295]

10—Mystery of the Divine Birth: Tasenetnofret and Panebtawy[296]

11—Birth of Ra and the Son of Shu and Tefnut (Mystery of the Divine Birth)[297]

---

[285] Siuda, Tamara L. The Ancient Egyptian Daybook. (Stargazer Design, 2016), 165.

[286] Siuda, Tamara L. The Ancient Egyptian Daybook. (Stargazer Design, 2016), 168.

[287] Siuda, Tamara L. The Ancient Egyptian Daybook. (Stargazer Design, 2016), 173 and 175.

[288] Siuda, Tamara L. The Ancient Egyptian Daybook. (Stargazer Design, 2016), 175.

[289] Siuda, Tamara L. The Ancient Egyptian Daybook. (Stargazer Design, 2016), 192.

[290] Siuda, Tamara L. The Ancient Egyptian Daybook. (Stargazer Design, 2016), 194.

[291] Siuda, Tamara L. The Ancient Egyptian Daybook. (Stargazer Design, 2016), 197.

[292] Siuda, Tamara L. The Ancient Egyptian Daybook. (Stargazer Design, 2016), 198.

[293] Siuda, Tamara L. The Ancient Egyptian Daybook. (Stargazer Design, 2016), 203.

[294] Siuda, Tamara L. The Ancient Egyptian Daybook. (Stargazer Design, 2016), 201-202. This festival celebrates the mother and child gods within the birth houses of temples. For this calendar, this festival pertains to Tefnut and Her son.

[295] Siuda, Tamara L. The Ancient Egyptian Daybook. (Stargazer Design, 2016), 208.

[296] Siuda, Tamara L. The Ancient Egyptian Daybook. (Stargazer Design, 2016), 201-202. This festival celebrates the mother and child gods within the birth houses of temples. Tasenetnofret can be either Tefnut or Hethert at Kom Ombo, but Hethert's son is Khonsu while Tefnut-Tasenetnofret's son is Panebtawy. Even though the text doesn's say Tefnut, I'm including it here for that reason.

[297] Siuda, Tamara L. The Ancient Egyptian Daybook. (Stargazer Design, 2016), 209.

12—Chronokrater: Onuris[298]
12—Chronokrater: Heru-Shu, Chosen by the Udjat[299]
18—Chronokrater: Onuris of Thinis[300]

1 Shomu/Pachons/April
1—Birthday of Shu and Tefnut at Philae[301]
1—Festival of Heru-Shu[302]
1—Appearance of Tasenetnofret[303]
6—Appearance of Tasenetnofret[304]
11 thru 20—Birthday of Shu and Tefnut (10 Days)[305]
New Moon Eve—Procession of Shu[306]

2 Shomu/Payni/May
14—Chronokrater: Onuris of the Retinue[307]
24—Chronokrater: Tefnut[308]
30—Procession of Shu to Retrieve the *Udjat* (Tefnut-Sekhmet): Dejhuty Calms Her[309]

3 Shomu/Epiphi/June
20 thru 22—Departure of the Wandering Eye Goddess (Solstice)[310]
29—Chronokrater: Onuris[311]

4 Shomu/Mesore/July

---

[298] Siuda, Tamara L. The Ancient Egyptian Daybook. (Stargazer Design, 2016), 210.
[299] Siuda, Tamara L. The Ancient Egyptian Daybook. (Stargazer Design, 2016), 210.
[300] Siuda, Tamara L. The Ancient Egyptian Daybook. (Stargazer Design, 2016), 212.
[301] Siuda, Tamara L. The Ancient Egyptian Daybook. (Stargazer Design, 2016), 225-226.
[302] Siuda, Tamara L. The Ancient Egyptian Daybook. (Stargazer Design, 2016), 225-226.
[303] Siuda, Tamara L. The Ancient Egyptian Daybook. (Stargazer Design, 2016), 225-226.
[304] Siuda, Tamara L. The Ancient Egyptian Daybook. (Stargazer Design, 2016), 229.
[305] Siuda, Tamara L. The Ancient Egyptian Daybook. (Stargazer Design, 2016), 231-236.
[306] Siuda, Tamara L. The Ancient Egyptian Daybook. (Stargazer Design, 2016), 312.
[307] Siuda, Tamara L. The Ancient Egyptian Daybook. (Stargazer Design, 2016), 250-251.
[308] Siuda, Tamara L. The Ancient Egyptian Daybook. (Stargazer Design, 2016), 254.
[309] Siuda, Tamara L. The Ancient Egyptian Daybook. (Stargazer Design, 2016), 257.
[310] Siuda, Tamara L. The Ancient Egyptian Daybook. (Stargazer Design, 2016), 140.
[311] Siuda, Tamara L. The Ancient Egyptian Daybook. (Stargazer Design, 2016), 274.

1–Appearance of Tasenetnofret[312]

6–Chronokrater: Tefnut[313]

19–Chronokrater: Tasenetnofret-Tefnut, She Who is Loved by Her Lord[314]

19–Chronokrater: Shu[315]

28–Chronokrater: Shu, Son of Atum[316]

---

[312] Siuda, Tamara L. The Ancient Egyptian Daybook. (Stargazer Design, 2016), 278-279.

[313] Siuda, Tamara L. The Ancient Egyptian Daybook. (Stargazer Design, 2016), 281.

[314] Siuda, Tamara L. The Ancient Egyptian Daybook. (Stargazer Design, 2016), 286.

[315] Siuda, Tamara L. The Ancient Egyptian Daybook. (Stargazer Design, 2016), 286.

[316] Siuda, Tamara L. The Ancient Egyptian Daybook. (Stargazer Design, 2016), 290.

THE GODDESS TEFNUT

Titles of Tefnut

Ancient Egyptian Names

- *Tasenetnofret*—Good Sister/Beautiful Sister[317]
- *Ruty*—Twin Lions of the Eastern and Western Horizons (with Shu)[318]
- *Wosret*—Powerful One[319]

Names in English

- All Who Were Near Her Feared Her Because of Her Power[320]
- Angry Lioness[321]
- Appearing in Senmet[322]
- Appears in Senmet for All Eternity[323]
- Apep Burns with Her Glowing Breath[324]
- At the Head of the House of Flame[325]

---

[317] Leitz, Christian, and Dagmar Budde, et. al. Lexikon der Ägyptischen Götter und Götterbezeichnungen (LGG, OLA 129, Band 8). (Peeters, 2003), 694.

[318] Tyldesley, Joyce. The Penguin Book of Myths and Legends of Ancient Egypt. (Penguin Books, 2011), 47.

[319] De Wit, Constant. Le rôle et le sens du lion dans l'Égypte ancienne. (Belgium: E.J. Brill, 1951), 330.

[320] West, Stephanie. "The Greek version of the legend of Tefnut." The Journal of Egyptian Archaeology 55, no. 1 (1969): 169.

[321] Leitz, Christian, and Dagmar Budde, et. al. Lexikon der Ägyptischen Götter und Götterbezeichnungen (LGG, OLA 129, Band 8). (Peeters, 2003), 700.

[322] Inconnu-Bocquillon, Danielle, Le mythe de la déesse lointaine à Philae, BdE 132, (Le Caire/Cairo: IFAO, 2001), 78.

[323] Kockelmann, Holger and Erich Winter, Philae III: Die Zweite Ostkolonnade des Tempels der Isis in Philae. (CO II und CO II K), (Verlag der Osterreichischen Akademie der Wissenschaften/Austrian Academy of Sciences, 2016), 189.

[324] Leitz, Christian. "Der grosse Repithymnus im Tempel von Athribis." In "Parcourir l'éternité", Hommages à Jean Yoyotte Bd. 2 (Bibliothèque de l'École des Hautes Études, Sciences Religieuses 156), Zivie-Coche, Christiane und Guermeur, Ivan (Hg.), (Turnhout 2012), 766.

- At the Site of Her Appearance in Memphis[326]
- At Whose Coming the Gods are Satisfied[327]
- At Whose Sight the Gods and Goddessess Rejoice[328]
- August[329]
- August and Perfect[330]
- August and Powerful[331]
- August and Venerable One[332]
- *Bau* of Heliopolis (with Shu)[333]
- Beautiful Cat[334]
- Beautiful North Wind[335]
- Beautiful One[336]
- Beautiful One Among the Gods[337]
- Beautiful Magnificent One[338]

---

[325] Inconnu-Bocquillon, Danielle, *Le mythe de la déesse lointaine à Philae*, BdE *132*, (Le Caire/Cairo: IFAO, 2001), 80.

[326] Verhoeven, Ursula. "Eine Vergewaltigung? Vom Umgang mit einer Textstelle des Naos von El Arish (Tefnut-Studien I)." Religion und Philosophie im Alten Ägypten, Festgabe für Philippe Derchain, Orientalia Lovaniensia Analecta 39, U. Verhoeven, E. Graefe (Hg.), Leuven 1991, 324.

[327] Leitz, Christian, and Dagmar Budde, et. al. Lexikon der Ägyptischen Götter und Götterbezeichnungen (LGG, OLA 129, Band 8). (Peeters, 2003), 701.

[328] Leitz, Christian, and Dagmar Budde, et. al. Lexikon der Ägyptischen Götter und Götterbezeichnungen (LGG, OLA 129, Band 8). (Peeters, 2003), 701.

[329] El-Tonssy, Mohamed A. "The Goddess Rattawy in the Greco-Roman Temples" الإلهة رعت تاوى فى معابد العصر اليونانى الرومانى. *The Conference Book of the General Union of Arab Archeologists*. *15*. (2012), pp. 195.

[330] Inconnu-Bocquillon, Danielle, *Le mythe de la déesse lointaine à Philae*, BdE *132*, (Le Caire/Cairo: IFAO, 2001), 45.

[331] Inconnu-Bocquillon, Danielle, *Le mythe de la déesse lointaine à Philae*, BdE *132*, (Le Caire/Cairo: IFAO, 2001), 22.

[332] Inconnu-Bocquillon, Danielle, *Le mythe de la déesse lointaine à Philae*, BdE *132*, (Le Caire/Cairo: IFAO, 2001), 86.

[333] Leitz, Christian, and Dagmar Budde, et. al. Lexikon der Ägyptischen Götter und Götterbezeichnungen (LGG, OLA 129, Band 8). (Peeters, 2003), 699.

[334] Spiegelberg, Wilhelm. *Der ägyptische Mythus vom Sonnenauge.* (Georg Olms Verlag, 1917), 3.

[335] Leitz, Christian, and Dagmar Budde, et. al. Lexikon der Ägyptischen Götter und Götterbezeichnungen (LGG, OLA 116, Band 7). (Peeters, 2002), 36-37.

[336] Leitz, Christian, and Dagmar Budde, et. al. Lexikon der Ägyptischen Götter und Götterbezeichnungen (LGG, OLA 129, Band 8). (Peeters, 2003), 702.

[337] Leitz, Christian, and Dagmar Budde, et. al. Lexikon der Ägyptischen Götter und Götterbezeichnungen (LGG, OLA 129, Band 8). (Peeters, 2003), 702.

- Beautiful Singer[339]
- Beautiful Sister[340]
- Beautiful Young Lioness[341]
- Beautiful Young Lioness of Heruakhety[342]
- Beauty on the Head of Her Father[343]
- Before Whose Terror People Escape[344]
- Before Whom No Other Existed[345]
- Both Eyes (with Shu)[346]
- Born of Ra[347]
- Burning Enemies with Her Burning Breath[348]
- Burning the Rebels with Her Scorching Breath[349]
- Cat[350]
- Cat of the Mistress of Heaven[351]
- Children of Heruakhety (with Shu)[352]

[338] Leitz, Christian, and Dagmar Budde, et. al. Lexikon der Ägyptischen Götter und Götterbezeichnungen (LGG, OLA 129, Band 8). (Peeters, 2003), 702.

[339] Leitz, Christian, and Dagmar Budde, et. al. Lexikon der Ägyptischen Götter und Götterbezeichnungen (LGG, OLA 129, Band 8). (Peeters, 2003), 701.

[340] Leitz, Christian, and Dagmar Budde, et. al. Lexikon der Ägyptischen Götter und Götterbezeichnungen (LGG, OLA 129, Band 8). (Peeters, 2003), 701.

[341] Leitz, Christian, and Dagmar Budde, et. al. Lexikon der Ägyptischen Götter und Götterbezeichnungen (LGG, OLA 129, Band 8). (Peeters, 2003), 700.

[342] Leitz, Christian, and Dagmar Budde, et. al. Lexikon der Ägyptischen Götter und Götterbezeichnungen (LGG, OLA 129, Band 8). (Peeters, 2003), 700.

[343] Inconnu-Bocquillon, Danielle, Le mythe de la déesse lointaine à Philae, BdE 132, (Le Caire/Cairo: IFAO, 2001), 23.

[344] Leitz, Christian, and Dagmar Budde, et. al. Lexikon der Ägyptischen Götter und Götterbezeichnungen (LGG, OLA 129, Band 8). (Peeters, 2003), 702.

[345] Leitz, Christian, and Dagmar Budde, et. al. Lexikon der Ägyptischen Götter und Götterbezeichnungen (LGG, OLA 129, Band 8). (Peeters, 2003), 700.

[346] Siuda, Tamara L. The Ancient Egyptian Daybook. (Stargazer Design, 2016), 155.

[347] Leitz, Christian, and Dagmar Budde, et. al. Lexikon der Ägyptischen Götter und Götterbezeichnungen (LGG, OLA 129, Band 8). (Peeters, 2003), 701.

[348] Inconnu-Bocquillon, Danielle, Le mythe de la déesse lointaine à Philae, BdE 132, (Le Caire/Cairo: IFAO, 2001), 83.

[349] Leitz, Christian, and Dagmar Budde, et. al. Lexikon der Ägyptischen Götter und Götterbezeichnungen (LGG, OLA 129, Band 8). (Peeters, 2003), 700.

[350] West, Stephanie. "The Greek version of the legend of Tefnut." The Journal of Egyptian Archaeology 55, no. 1 (1969): 178.

[351] Spiegelberg, Wilhelm. Der ägyptische Mythus vom Sonnenauge. (Georg Olms Verlag, 1917), 3.

- Cobra[353]
- Cobra of Bubastis[354]
- Cobra of Edfu[355]
- Cobra of All Gods[356]
- Cobra of Every God[357]
- Cobra of Her Father[358]
- Cobra of the One Who Created Her[359]
- Cobra of Ra[360]
- Coiled One on the Head of Her Father[361]
- Confidante of Her Creator[362]
- Confidante of Her Father[363]
- Consort of the Gods[364]
- Children of the Cobra-Snake (with Shu)[365]
- Crown of the Solar Disk[366]

---

[352] Leitz, Christian, and Dagmar Budde, et. al. Lexikon der Ägyptischen Götter und Götterbezeichnungen (LGG, OLA 129, Band 8). (Peeters, 2003), 701.

[353] Leitz, Christian, and Dagmar Budde, et. al. Lexikon der Ägyptischen Götter und Götterbezeichnungen (LGG, OLA 129, Band 8). (Peeters, 2003), 700.

[354] Leitz, Christian, and Dagmar Budde, et. al. Lexikon der Ägyptischen Götter und Götterbezeichnungen (LGG, OLA 129, Band 8). (Peeters, 2003), 699.

[355] Leitz, Christian, and Dagmar Budde, et. al. Lexikon der Ägyptischen Götter und Götterbezeichnungen (LGG, OLA 129, Band 8). (Peeters, 2003), 699.

[356] Leitz, Christian, and Dagmar Budde, et. al. Lexikon der Ägyptischen Götter und Götterbezeichnungen (LGG, OLA 129, Band 8). (Peeters, 2003), 700.

[357] Leitz, Christian, and Dagmar Budde, et. al. Lexikon der Ägyptischen Götter und Götterbezeichnungen (LGG, OLA 129, Band 8). (Peeters, 2003), 700.

[358] Leitz, Christian, and Dagmar Budde, et. al. Lexikon der Ägyptischen Götter und Götterbezeichnungen (LGG, OLA 129, Band 8). (Peeters, 2003), 700.

[359] Leitz, Christian, and Dagmar Budde, et. al. Lexikon der Ägyptischen Götter und Götterbezeichnungen (LGG, OLA 129, Band 8). (Peeters, 2003), 700.

[360] Leitz, Christian, and Dagmar Budde, et. al. Lexikon der Ägyptischen Götter und Götterbezeichnungen (LGG, OLA 129, Band 8). (Peeters, 2003), 700.

[361] Inconnu-Bocquillon, Danielle, *Le mythe de la déesse lointaine à Philae, BdE 132*, (Le Caire/Cairo: IFAO, 2001), 43.

[362] Leitz, Christian, and Dagmar Budde, et. al. Lexikon der Ägyptischen Götter und Götterbezeichnungen (LGG, OLA 129, Band 8). (Peeters, 2003), 701.

[363] Leitz, Christian, and Dagmar Budde, et. al. Lexikon der Ägyptischen Götter und Götterbezeichnungen (LGG, OLA 129, Band 8). (Peeters, 2003), 701.

[364] Siuda, Tamara L. The Ancient Egyptian Daybook. (Stargazer Design, 2016), 116-117.

[365] Merkelbach, Reinhold. *Isis Regina-Zeus Sarapis: die griechisch-ägyptische Religion nach den Quellen dargestellt.* (Walter de Gruyter, 2012), 34.

- Daughter of Atum[367]
- Daughter of Ra[368]
- Daughter of Ra in the Beautiful Place[369]
- Daughter of Ra in Dendera[370]
- Daughter of Ra in the House of the Beginning[371]
- Daughter of Ra in the House of Philae[372]
- Daughter of Ra in Iatdi[373]
- Daughter of Ra in the Nome of the Beginning[374]
- Daughter of Ra in Philae[375]
- Daughter of Ra in Senmet[376]
- Daughter of Ra on the Abaton[377]
- Daughter of Ra on the Throne of Ra[378]
- Daughter of Ra, Sovereign in Bugem[379]

---

[366] Cauville, Sylvie. Dendara V-VI: II: Index Phraseologique. (Belgium: Peeters, 2004), 360.

[367] Leitz, Christian, and Dagmar Budde, et. al. Lexikon der Ägyptischen Götter und Götterbezeichnungen (LGG, OLA 129, Band 8). (Peeters, 2003), 701.

[368] Preys, René. Les complexes de la Demeure du Sistre et du Trône de Rê: théologie et décoration dans le temple d'Hathor à Dendera. Vol. 106. (Peeters Publishers, 2002), 205.

[369] Leitz, Christian, and Dagmar Budde, et. al. Lexikon der Ägyptischen Götter und Götterbezeichnungen (LGG, OLA 129, Band 8). (Peeters, 2003), 699.

[370] Gaber, Amr. "The Central Hall in the Egyptian Temples of the Ptolemaic Period." (PhD diss., Durham University, 2009), 154.

[371] Leitz, Christian, and Dagmar Budde, et. al. Lexikon der Ägyptischen Götter und Götterbezeichnungen (LGG, OLA 129, Band 8). (Peeters, 2003), 699.

[372] Leitz, Christian, and Dagmar Budde, et. al. Lexikon der Ägyptischen Götter und Götterbezeichnungen (LGG, OLA 129, Band 8). (Peeters, 2003), 699.

[373] Cauville, Sylvie. Dendara II: Traduction. (Belgium: Uitgeverij Peeters, 1999), 367. Gaber, Amr. "The Central Hall in the Egyptian Temples of the Ptolemaic Period." (PhD diss., Durham University, 2009), 259.

[374] El-Tonssy, Mohamed A. "The Goddess Rattawy in the Greco-Roman Temples" الإلهة رعت تاوى فى معابد العصر اليونانى الرومانى. The Conference Book of the General Union of Arab Archeologists. 15. (2012), pp. 195.

[375] Kockelmann, Holger and Erich Winter, Philae III: Die Zweite Ostkolonnade des Tempels der Isis in Philae. (CO II und CO II K), (Verlag der Osterreichischen Akademie der Wissenschaften/Austrian Academy of Sciences, 2016), 141.

[376] Leitz, Christian, and Dagmar Budde, et. al. Lexikon der Ägyptischen Götter und Götterbezeichnungen (LGG, OLA 129, Band 8). (Peeters, 2003), 699.

[377] Kockelmann, Holger and Erich Winter, Philae III: Die Zweite Ostkolonnade des Tempels der Isis in Philae. (CO II und CO II K), (Verlag der Osterreichischen Akademie der Wissenschaften/Austrian Academy of Sciences, 2016), 231.

[378] Leitz, Christian, and Dagmar Budde, et. al. Lexikon der Ägyptischen Götter und Götterbezeichnungen (LGG, OLA 129, Band 8). (Peeters, 2003), 699.

- Daughter of Ra, Who Loves Her[380]
- Daughter of Ra, Whom He Likes to See[381]
- Daughter of Ra, Whom Her Heart Loves[382]
- Daughter of the Sun[383]
- Destroying Her Opponents as She Does in the Necropolis[384]
- Devourer of Fire[385]
- Devouring Flame[386]
- Diadem on His Forehead[387]
- Divine Mother[388]
- Divine Sister of Shu[389]
- Divine Wife[390]
- Dorkas Gazelle of the Desert[391]
- Dwelling in Elephantine[392]

---

[379] Richter, Barbara A. "On the Heels of the Wandering Goddess: The Myth and the Festival at the Temples of the Wadi el-Hallel and Dendera." Dolinska, Monika and Beinlich, Horst (eds.) 8. Ägyptologische Tempeltagung: interconnections between temples : Warschau, 22.-25. September 2008. Germany: Harrassowitz, 2010: 167.

[380] Inconnu-Bocquillon, Danielle, *Le mythe de la déesse lointaine à Philae*, BdE 132, (Le Caire/Cairo: IFAO, 2001), 88.

[381] Cauville, Sylvie., Lecler, Alain. Dendara I: Traduction. (Belgium: Peeters, 1998), 137.

[382] Inconnu-Bocquillon, Danielle, *Le mythe de la déesse lointaine à Philae*, BdE 132, (Le Caire/Cairo: IFAO, 2001), 78.

[383] Piehl, Karl. Inscriptions hiéroglyphiques recueillies en Égypte. (Germany: n.p., 1890), 99.

[384] Piehl, Karl. Inscriptions hiéroglyphiques recueillies en Égypte. (Germany: n.p., 1890), 64.

[385] Leitz, Christian, and Dagmar Budde, et. al. Lexikon der Ägyptischen Götter und Götterbezeichnungen (LGG, OLA 129, Band 8). (Peeters, 2003), 700.

[386] Spiegelberg, Wilhelm. *Der ägyptische Mythus vom Sonnenauge*. (Georg Olms Verlag, 1917), 34, footnote 6. This is for Hethert, Tefnut, Bast and Sekhmet.

[387] Piehl, Karl. Inscriptions hiéroglyphiques recueillies en Égypte. (Germany: n.p., 1890), 96.

[388] Preys, René. *Les complexes de la Demeure du Sistre et du Trône de Rê: théologie et décoration dans le temple d'Hathor à Dendera*. Vol. 106. (Peeters Publishers, 2002), 205.

[389] Leitz, Christian, and Dagmar Budde, et. al. Lexikon der Ägyptischen Götter und Götterbezeichnungen (LGG, OLA 129, Band 8). (Peeters, 2003), 701.

[390] Leitz, Christian, and Dagmar Budde, et. al. Lexikon der Ägyptischen Götter und Götterbezeichnungen (LGG, OLA 129, Band 8). (Peeters, 2003), 701.

[391] Leitz, Christian, and Dagmar Budde, et. al. Lexikon der Ägyptischen Götter und Götterbezeichnungen (LGG, OLA 129, Band 8). (Peeters, 2003), 699.

- Embodiment of Death[393]
- Embodiment of Retribution and Revenge[394]
- Ethiopian Cat[395]
- Ethiopian Cat, Daughter of Ra, Mistress of the Uraeus[396]
- Eye of Atum[397]
- Eye of Ra[398]
- Eye of Ra in Dendera[399]
- Eye of Ra in Iatdi (Temple of Aset in Dendera)[400]
- Eye of Ra in Iunet[401]
- Eye of the Sun[402]
- Excellent One[403]
- Excellent Burning One[404]
- Female *Ba* Greater than the Gods[405]

---

[392] Kockelmann, Holger and Erich Winter, *Philae III: Die Zweite Ostkolonnade des Tempels der Isis in Philae. (CO II und CO II K)*, (Verlag der Osterreichischen Akademie der Wissenschaften/Austrian Academy of Sciences, 2016), 189.

[393] Leitz, Christian, and Dagmar Budde, et. al. Lexikon der Ägyptischen Götter und Götterbezeichnungen (LGG, OLA 129, Band 8). (Peeters, 2003), 700.

[394] Leitz, Christian, and Dagmar Budde, et. al. Lexikon der Ägyptischen Götter und Götterbezeichnungen (LGG, OLA 129, Band 8). (Peeters, 2003), 702.

[395] West, Stephanie. "The Greek version of the legend of Tefnut." *The Journal of Egyptian Archaeology* 55, no. 1 (1969): 178.

[396] Spiegelberg, Wilhelm. *Der ägyptische Mythus vom Sonnenauge.* (Georg Olms Verlag, 1917), 2.

[397] Tyldesley, Joyce. The Penguin Book of Myths and Legends of Ancient Egypt. (Penguin Books, 2011), 48.

[398] Inconnu-Bocquillon, Danielle, *Le mythe de la déesse lointaine à Philae, BdE 132*, (Le Caire/Cairo: IFAO, 2001), 23.

[399] Leitz, Christian, and Dagmar Budde, et. al. Lexikon der Ägyptischen Götter und Götterbezeichnungen (LGG, OLA 129, Band 8). (Peeters, 2003), 698.

[400] Leitz, Christian, and Dagmar Budde, et. al. Lexikon der Ägyptischen Götter und Götterbezeichnungen (LGG, OLA 129, Band 8). (Peeters, 2003), 699.

[401] Cauville, Sylvie. Dendara V-VI: II: Index Phraseologique. (Belgium: Peeters, 2004), 172.

[402] Piehl, Karl. Inscriptions hiéroglyphiques recueillies en Égypte. (Germany: n.p., 1890), 96.

[403] Leitz, Christian, and Dagmar Budde, et. al. Lexikon der Ägyptischen Götter und Götterbezeichnungen (LGG, OLA 129, Band 8). (Peeters, 2003), 702.

[404] Leitz, Christian, and Dagmar Budde, et. al. Lexikon der Ägyptischen Götter und Götterbezeichnungen (LGG, OLA 129, Band 8). (Peeters, 2003), 700.

[405] Inconnu-Bocquillon, Danielle, *Le mythe de la déesse lointaine à Philae, BdE 132*, (Le Caire/Cairo: IFAO, 2001), 50.

- Female Disk[406]
- Female Gazelle of the Mountain[407]
- Female Ra[408]
- Flame[409]
- Flame and Powerful[410]
- Flame in Her Moment[411]
- Flaming One[412]
- Flame, Who Burns Her Enemies[413]
- Flame, Who Shoots Out[414]
- Fire[415]
- Fire-Breathing Lioness[416]
- First Daughter of the Ancestors[417]
- First Daughter of Atum[418]
- First Goddess[419]

---

[406] Husson, Constance. L'offrande du miroir dans les temples égyptiens de l'époque gréco-romaine. (France: Audin, 1977), 159.

[407] Strandberg, Åsa. The Gazelle in Ancient Egyptian Art: Image and Meaning. (Sweden: University of Uppsala. Department of Archaeology and Ancient History, 2009), 183.

[408] Inconnu-Bocquillon, Danielle, *Le mythe de la déesse lointaine à Philae*, BdE 132, (Le Caire/Cairo: IFAO, 2001), 22.

[409] Inconnu-Bocquillon, Danielle, *Le mythe de la déesse lointaine à Philae*, BdE 132, (Le Caire/Cairo: IFAO, 2001), 83.

[410] Cauville, Sylvie. Dendara V-VI: II: Index Phraseologique. (Belgium: Peeters, 2004), 119.

[411] Leitz, Christian, and Dagmar Budde, et. al. Lexikon der Ägyptischen Götter und Götterbezeichnungen (LGG, OLA 129, Band 8). (Peeters, 2003), 702.

[412] Leitz, Christian, and Dagmar Budde, et. al. Lexikon der Ägyptischen Götter und Götterbezeichnungen (LGG, OLA 129, Band 8). (Peeters, 2003), 702.

[413] Inconnu-Bocquillon, Danielle, *Le mythe de la déesse lointaine à Philae*, BdE 132, (Le Caire/Cairo: IFAO, 2001), 86.

[414] Inconnu-Bocquillon, Danielle, *Le mythe de la déesse lointaine à Philae*, BdE 132, (Le Caire/Cairo: IFAO, 2001), 78.

[415] Piehl, Karl. Inscriptions hiéroglyphiques recueillies en Égypte. (Germany: n.p., 1890), 64.

[416] Tyldesley, Joyce. The Penguin Book of Myths and Legends of Ancient Egypt. (Penguin Books, 2011), 51.

[417] Leitz, Christian, and Dagmar Budde, et. al. Lexikon der Ägyptischen Götter und Götterbezeichnungen (LGG, OLA 129, Band 8). (Peeters, 2003), 701.

[418] Leitz, Christian, and Dagmar Budde, et. al. Lexikon der Ägyptischen Götter und Götterbezeichnungen (LGG, OLA 129, Band 8). (Peeters, 2003), 701.

[419] Leitz, Christian, and Dagmar Budde, et. al. Lexikon der Ägyptischen Götter und Götterbezeichnungen (LGG, OLA 129, Band 8). (Peeters, 2003), 702.

- Forehead Snake on the Earth[420]
- Foremost of the Beautiful House[421]
- Foremost of Edfu[422]
- Foremost of the Ennead[423]
- Foremost of the Goddesses[424]
- Foremost of the Great Throne[425]
- Foremost of the Hills of Tefnut[426]
- Foremost of the House of the Falcon[427]
- Foremost of the House of the Figures/Statues[428]
- Foremost of the House of the Two Children[429]
- Foremost of Iatdi (Temple of Aset in Dendera)[430]
- Foremost of the Land of Atum[431]
- Foremost of the Nomes at the Beginning[432]
- Foremost of the Palace of Nobility[433]

---

[420] Leitz, Christian, and Dagmar Budde, et. al. Lexikon der Ägyptischen Götter und Götterbezeichnungen (LGG, OLA 129, Band 8). (Peeters, 2003), 698.
[421] Leitz, Christian, and Dagmar Budde, et. al. Lexikon der Ägyptischen Götter und Götterbezeichnungen (LGG, OLA 129, Band 8). (Peeters, 2003), 699.
[422] Leitz, Christian, and Dagmar Budde, et. al. Lexikon der Ägyptischen Götter und Götterbezeichnungen (LGG, OLA 129, Band 8). (Peeters, 2003), 699.
[423] Leitz, Christian, and Dagmar Budde, et. al. Lexikon der Ägyptischen Götter und Götterbezeichnungen (LGG, OLA 129, Band 8). (Peeters, 2003), 702.
[424] Leitz, Christian, and Dagmar Budde, et. al. Lexikon der Ägyptischen Götter und Götterbezeichnungen (LGG, OLA 129, Band 8). (Peeters, 2003), 702.
[425] Leitz, Christian, and Dagmar Budde, et. al. Lexikon der Ägyptischen Götter und Götterbezeichnungen (LGG, OLA 129, Band 8). (Peeters, 2003), 699.
[426] Leitz, Christian, and Dagmar Budde, et. al. Lexikon der Ägyptischen Götter und Götterbezeichnungen (LGG, OLA 129, Band 8). (Peeters, 2003), 699.
[427] Leitz, Christian, and Dagmar Budde, et. al. Lexikon der Ägyptischen Götter und Götterbezeichnungen (LGG, OLA 129, Band 8). (Peeters, 2003), 699.
[428] Leitz, Christian, and Dagmar Budde, et. al. Lexikon der Ägyptischen Götter und Götterbezeichnungen (LGG, OLA 129, Band 8). (Peeters, 2003), 699.
[429] Leitz, Christian, and Dagmar Budde, et. al. Lexikon der Ägyptischen Götter und Götterbezeichnungen (LGG, OLA 129, Band 8). (Peeters, 2003), 699.
[430] Leitz, Christian, and Dagmar Budde, et. al. Lexikon der Ägyptischen Götter und Götterbezeichnungen (LGG, OLA 129, Band 8). (Peeters, 2003), 699.
[431] Leitz, Christian, and Dagmar Budde, et. al. Lexikon der Ägyptischen Götter und Götterbezeichnungen (LGG, OLA 129, Band 8). (Peeters, 2003), 699.
[432] Leitz, Christian, and Dagmar Budde, et. al. Lexikon der Ägyptischen Götter und Götterbezeichnungen (LGG, OLA 129, Band 8). (Peeters, 2003), 698.

- Foremost of Philae[434]
- Foremost of Senmet[435]
- Foremost of the Temple of Ra[436]
- Foremost of the Throne of the Gods (Edfu)[437]
- Foremost of the Throne of Ra[438]
- Gazelle of the Desert[439]
- Goddess[440]
- Goddess, Mother and Daughter (with Aset)[441]
- Goddess in Senmet[442]
- Gods Who Created the Primordial Gods (with Shu)[443]
- Great[444]
- Great of Carnage[445]
- Great of Carnage on the Place of Execution[446]

[433] Leitz, Christian, and Dagmar Budde, et. al. Lexikon der Ägyptischen Götter und Götterbezeichnungen (LGG, OLA 129, Band 8). (Peeters, 2003), 699.

[434] Leitz, Christian, and Dagmar Budde, et. al. Lexikon der Ägyptischen Götter und Götterbezeichnungen (LGG, OLA 129, Band 8). (Peeters, 2003), 699.

[435] Leitz, Christian, and Dagmar Budde, et. al. Lexikon der Ägyptischen Götter und Götterbezeichnungen (LGG, OLA 129, Band 8). (Peeters, 2003), 699.

[436] Leitz, Christian, and Dagmar Budde, et. al. Lexikon der Ägyptischen Götter und Götterbezeichnungen (LGG, OLA 129, Band 8). (Peeters, 2003), 699.

[437] Leitz, Christian, and Dagmar Budde, et. al. Lexikon der Ägyptischen Götter und Götterbezeichnungen (LGG, OLA 129, Band 8). (Peeters, 2003), 699.

[438] Leitz, Christian, and Dagmar Budde, et. al. Lexikon der Ägyptischen Götter und Götterbezeichnungen (LGG, OLA 129, Band 8). (Peeters, 2003), 699.

[439] Spiegelberg, Wilhelm. *Der ägyptische Mythus vom Sonnenauge.* (Georg Olms Verlag, 1917), 52, footnote 7.

[440] Siuda, Tamara L. The Ancient Egyptian Daybook. (Stargazer Design, 2016), 63-66.

[441] Goyon, Jean-Claude. "Inscriptions Tardives Du Temple De Mout à Karnak." *Journal of the American Research Center in Egypt* 20 (1983): 56-57.

[442] Kockelmann, Holger and Erich Winter, *Philae III: Die Zweite Ostkolonnade des Tempels der Isis in Philae. (CO II und CO II K),* (Verlag der Osterreichischen Akademie der Wissenschaften/Austrian Academy of Sciences, 2016), 141.

[443] De Wit, Constant. *Le rôle et le sens du lion dans l'Égypte ancienne.* (Belgium: E.J. Brill, 1951), 178.

[444] Leitz, Christian, and Dagmar Budde, et. al. Lexikon der Ägyptischen Götter und Götterbezeichnungen (LGG, OLA 129, Band 8). (Peeters, 2003), 702. From transliteration of the hieroglyphs.

[445] Inconnu-Bocquillon, Danielle, *Le mythe de la déesse lointaine à Philae, BdE 132,* (Le Caire/Cairo: IFAO, 2001), 50.

- Great of Love[447]
- Great of Love in the Heart of Her Father[448]
- Great of Magic[449]
- Great Burning One with Her Brother[450]
- Great Cobra[451]
- Great Daughter of Ra[452]
- Great Goddess[453]
- Great Magnificent One of Bugem[454]
- Great in Millions[455]
- Great Flame[456]
- Great Flame Goddess[457]
- Great Flame in the Castle of Flame[458]

---

[446] Inconnu-Bocquillon, Danielle, *Le mythe de la déesse lointaine à Philae*, BdE 132, (Le Caire/Cairo: IFAO, 2001), 50.

[447] Leitz, Christian, and Dagmar Budde, et. al. Lexikon der Ägyptischen Götter und Götterbezeichnungen (LGG, OLA 129, Band 8). (Peeters, 2003), 701. From transliteration of the hieroglyphs.

[448] Leitz, Christian, and Dagmar Budde, et. al. Lexikon der Ägyptischen Götter und Götterbezeichnungen (LGG, OLA 129, Band 8). (Peeters, 2003), 701. From transliteration of the hieroglyphs.

[449] Leitz, Christian, and Dagmar Budde, et. al. Lexikon der Ägyptischen Götter und Götterbezeichnungen (LGG, OLA 129, Band 8). (Peeters, 2003), 702.

[450] Leitz, Christian, and Dagmar Budde, et. al. Lexikon der Ägyptischen Götter und Götterbezeichnungen (LGG, OLA 129, Band 8). (Peeters, 2003), 701.

[451] Leitz, Christian, and Dagmar Budde, et. al. Lexikon der Ägyptischen Götter und Götterbezeichnungen (LGG, OLA 129, Band 8). (Peeters, 2003), 700.

[452] El-Tonssy, Mohamed A. "The Goddess Rattawy in the Greco-Roman Temples" الإلهة رعت تاوى فى معابد العصر اليونانى الرومانى. *The Conference Book of the General Union of Arab Archeologists*. 15. (2012), pp. 195.

[453] Leitz, Christian, and Dagmar Budde, et. al. Lexikon der Ägyptischen Götter und Götterbezeichnungen (LGG, OLA 129, Band 8). (Peeters, 2003), 702. From transliteration of the hieroglyphs.

[454] Leitz, Christian, and Dagmar Budde, et. al. Lexikon der Ägyptischen Götter und Götterbezeichnungen (LGG, OLA 129, Band 8). (Peeters, 2003), 699.

[455] Siuda, Tamara L. The Ancient Egyptian Daybook. (Stargazer Design, 2016), 198. To Tefnut-Sekhmet/Sekhmet-Tefnut.

[456] Kockelmann, Holger and Erich Winter, *Philae III: Die Zweite Ostkolonnade des Tempels der Isis in Philae. (CO II und CO II K)*, (Verlag der Osterreichischen Akademie der Wissenschaften/Austrian Academy of Sciences, 2016), 141.

[457] Kockelmann, Holger and Erich Winter, *Philae III: Die Zweite Ostkolonnade des Tempels der Isis in Philae. (CO II und CO II K)*, (Verlag der Osterreichischen Akademie der Wissenschaften/Austrian Academy of Sciences, 2016), 231.

- Great Flame in Senmet[459]
- Great Flame Surrounding Him[460]
- Great Flaming One[461]
- Great One Embracing Her Brother Shu[462]
- Great One of the Underworld[463]
- Great Primordial One[464]
- Great Recipient/Unifier[465]
- Great Royal Bride[466]
- Great Rulers (with Shu)[467]
- Great Secret One[468]
- Great Sovereign in the Chapel[469]
- Great *Uraeus*[470]
- Great *Uraeus* in Dendera[471]

---

[458] Inconnu-Bocquillon, Danielle, *Le mythe de la déesse lointaine à Philae, BdE 132*, (Le Caire/Cairo: IFAO, 2001), 51.

[459] Leitz, Christian, and Dagmar Budde, et. al. Lexikon der Ägyptischen Götter und Götterbezeichnungen (LGG, OLA 129, Band 8). (Peeters, 2003), 699.

[460] Inconnu-Bocquillon, Danielle, *Le mythe de la déesse lointaine à Philae, BdE 132*, (Le Caire/Cairo: IFAO, 2001), 57.

[461] Leitz, Christian, and Dagmar Budde, et. al. Lexikon der Ägyptischen Götter und Götterbezeichnungen (LGG, OLA 129, Band 8). (Peeters, 2003), 702.

[462] Leitz, Christian, and Dagmar Budde, et. al. Lexikon der Ägyptischen Götter und Götterbezeichnungen (LGG, OLA 129, Band 8). (Peeters, 2003), 701.

[463] Leitz, Christian, and Dagmar Budde, et. al. Lexikon der Ägyptischen Götter und Götterbezeichnungen (LGG, OLA 129, Band 8). (Peeters, 2003), 698.

[464] Leitz, Christian, and Dagmar Budde, et. al. Lexikon der Ägyptischen Götter und Götterbezeichnungen (LGG, OLA 129, Band 8). (Peeters, 2003), 700.

[465] Leitz, Christian, and Dagmar Budde, et. al. Lexikon der Ägyptischen Götter und Götterbezeichnungen (LGG, OLA 129, Band 8). (Peeters, 2003), 700.

[466] Mancini, Mattia. "Tefnut l'eliopolitana ad Amarna." *Egitto e Vicino Oriente* 39 (2016): 53. Along with Queen Nefertiti.

[467] Leitz, Christian, and Dagmar Budde, et. al. Lexikon der Ägyptischen Götter und Götterbezeichnungen (LGG, OLA 129, Band 8). (Peeters, 2003), 701.

[468] Leitz, Christian, and Dagmar Budde, et. al. Lexikon der Ägyptischen Götter und Götterbezeichnungen (LGG, OLA 129, Band 8). (Peeters, 2003), 702.

[469] Inconnu-Bocquillon, Danielle, *Le mythe de la déesse lointaine à Philae, BdE 132*, (Le Caire/Cairo: IFAO, 2001), 22.

[470] Leitz, Christian, and Dagmar Budde, et. al. Lexikon der Ägyptischen Götter und Götterbezeichnungen (LGG, OLA 129, Band 8). (Peeters, 2003), 700.

[471] Leitz, Christian, and Dagmar Budde, et. al. Lexikon der Ägyptischen Götter und Götterbezeichnungen (LGG, OLA 129, Band 8). (Peeters, 2003), 699.

- Great *Uraeus* of the Lord of All[472]
- Great *Uraeus* on the Head of Her Father[473]
- Great *Uraeus* on the Head of Ra[474]
- Great Wepeset[475]
- Greatly Beloved Daughter[476]
- Grim-Faced Woman Among the Enemies of Her Father[477]
- Hand of God[478]
- Her Back Had the Color of Blood[479]
- Her Body is Hidden More Than the Gods[480]
- Her Daughter Tefnut (daughter is Aset here)[481]
- Her Eyes Blazed Like Flame[482]
- Her Eyes Blazed Like Flame, Throwing Fire Like the Sun at Noon[483]
- Her Eyes Glowed Like Fire[484]

[472] Leitz, Christian, and Dagmar Budde, et. al. Lexikon der Ägyptischen Götter und Götterbezeichnungen (LGG, OLA 129, Band 8). (Peeters, 2003), 700.
[473] Leitz, Christian, and Dagmar Budde, et. al. Lexikon der Ägyptischen Götter und Götterbezeichnungen (LGG, OLA 129, Band 8). (Peeters, 2003), 700.
[474] Leitz, Christian, and Dagmar Budde, et. al. Lexikon der Ägyptischen Götter und Götterbezeichnungen (LGG, OLA 129, Band 8). (Peeters, 2003), 700.
[475] Hölbl, Günther. Altägypten im Römischen Reich: Die Tempel des römischen Nubien. Vol. 2. (Zabern, 2004), 143.
[476] Pinch, Geraldine. Egyptian Mythology: A Guide to the Gods, Goddesses and Traditions of Ancient Egypt. (New York: Oxford University Press, 2004), 197.
[477] Leitz, Christian, and Dagmar Budde, et. al. Lexikon der Ägyptischen Götter und Götterbezeichnungen (LGG, OLA 129, Band 8). (Peeters, 2003), 701.
[478] Goyon, Jean-Claude. "Inscriptions Tardives Du Temple De Mout à Karnak." *Journal of the American Research Center in Egypt* 20 (1983): 56-57. Mut-Tefnut-Aset.
[479] West, Stephanie. "The Greek version of the legend of Tefnut." *The Journal of Egyptian Archaeology* 55, no. 1 (1969): 169.
[480] El-Tonssy, Mohamed A. "The Goddess Rattawy in the Greco-Roman Temples" الإلهة رعت تاوى فى معابد العصر اليونانى الرومانى. *The Conference Book of the General Union of Arab Archeologists*. 15. (2012), pp. 195.
[481] Goedicke, Hans. Die Darstellung des Horus: ein Mysterienspiel in Philae unter Ptolemäus VIII. (Verbandes der wissenschaftlichen Gesellschaften Österreichs, 1982), 119. The daughter is identified later in the text as Aset.
[482] West, Stephanie. "The Greek version of the legend of Tefnut." *The Journal of Egyptian Archaeology* 55, no. 1 (1969): 169.
[483] West, Stephanie. "The Greek version of the legend of Tefnut." *The Journal of Egyptian Archaeology* 55, no. 1 (1969): 169.

- Her Face Glinting Like the Sun's Disk[485]
- Her Father Rejoices to See Her[486]
- Her Father Ra Rejoices at the Sight of Her[487]
- Her Fur Smoked from Fire[488]
- Higher than the Goddesses[489]
- Image of Atum[490]
- In the Arms of Aker[491]
- In the Company of Her Brother[492]
- In Her Beauiful Form[493]
- In Her Beautiful Form as Tefnut[494]
- In Iunet (Dendera)[495]
- In the Mound of Tefnut[496]
- In Her Name of Menhyt-Nebetuu[497]

---

[484] West, Stephanie. "The Greek version of the legend of Tefnut." *The Journal of Egyptian Archaeology* 55, no. 1 (1969): 169.

[485] West, Stephanie. "The Greek version of the legend of Tefnut." *The Journal of Egyptian Archaeology* 55, no. 1 (1969): 169.

[486] Inconnu-Bocquillon, Danielle, *Le mythe de la déesse lointaine à Philae, BdE 132*, (Le Caire/Cairo: IFAO, 2001), 88.

[487] Leitz, Christian, and Dagmar Budde, et. al. Lexikon der Ägyptischen Götter und Götterbezeichnungen (LGG, OLA 129, Band 8). (Peeters, 2003), 701.

[488] West, Stephanie. "The Greek version of the legend of Tefnut." *The Journal of Egyptian Archaeology* 55, no. 1 (1969): 169.

[489] Inconnu-Bocquillon, Danielle, *Le mythe de la déesse lointaine à Philae, BdE 132*, (Le Caire/Cairo: IFAO, 2001), 50.

[490] Leitz, Christian, and Dagmar Budde, et. al. Lexikon der Ägyptischen Götter und Götterbezeichnungen (LGG, OLA 129, Band 8). (Peeters, 2003), 702.

[491] De Wit, Constant. *Le rôle et le sens du lion dans l'Égypte ancienne.* (Belgium: E.J. Brill, 1951), 100.

[492] Inconnu-Bocquillon, Danielle, *Le mythe de la déesse lointaine à Philae, BdE 132*, (Le Caire/Cairo: IFAO, 2001), 61.

[493] Spiegelberg, Wilhelm. *Der ägyptische Mythus vom Sonnenauge.* (Georg Olms Verlag, 1917), 53.

[494] Spiegelberg, Wilhelm. *Der ägyptische Mythus vom Sonnenauge.* (Georg Olms Verlag, 1917), 8.

[495] Lafont, Julie. "Consommation et proscription du miel en Égypte ancienne. Quand bj.t devient bw.t," in *BIFAO 116* (2016), p. 102.

[496] Cauville, Sylvie. Dendara II: Traduction. (Belgium: Uitgeverij Peeters, 1999), 367.

[497] Sauneron, Serge, *Esna V: Les fêtes religieuses d'Esna aux derniers siècles du paganisme,* (Cairo: IFAO, 1962; 2004), 89. Within a hymn to Khnum. Translated by Chelsea Bolton.

- In the Midst of the Abaton[498]
- In the Thinite Nome[499]
- In Whose Vicinity is the Great Flame[500]
- *Ka* and *Kat* (life-force/womb) (with Shu)[501]
- Lady of the Abaton[502]
- Lady of the Angry Glance[503]
- Lady of the Disk in Iatdi[504]
- Lady of Faience[505]
- Lady of Flame[506]
- Lady of Flame in the Castle of Flame[507]
- Lady of Flame in the House of Flame[508]
- Lady of Heaven[509]
- Lady of Hermopolis Parva[510]

---

[498] Kockelmann, Holger and Erich Winter, *Philae III: Die Zweite Ostkolonnade des Tempels der Isis in Philae. (CO II und CO II K)*, (Verlag der Osterreichischen Akademie der Wissenschaften/Austrian Academy of Sciences, 2016), 292.

[499] Brand, Peter J., Rosa Erika Feleg and William J. Murnane. The Great Hypostyle Hall in the Temple of Amun at Karnak: Vol 1, Part 2: Translation and Commentary. (Chicago: Oriental Institute of the University of Chicago, 2018), 314.

[500] Kockelmann, Holger and Erich Winter, *Philae III: Die Zweite Ostkolonnade des Tempels der Isis in Philae. (CO II und CO II K)*, (Verlag der Osterreichischen Akademie der Wissenschaften/Austrian Academy of Sciences, 2016), 189.

[501] Lekov, Teodor. "The Role of the Ka in the Process of Creation and Birth." *Journal of Egyptological Studies* 4 (2015): 34.

[502] Inconnu-Bocquillon, Danielle, *Le mythe de la déesse lointaine à Philae, BdE 132*, (Le Caire/Cairo: IFAO, 2001), 57.

[503] Siuda, Tamara L. The Ancient Egyptian Daybook. (Stargazer Design, 2016), 97.

[504] Husson, Constance. L'offrande du miroir dans les temples égyptiens de l'époque gréco-romaine. (France: Audin, 1977), 159.

[505] Siuda, Tamara L. The Ancient Egyptian Daybook. (Stargazer Design, 2016), 175.

[506] Inconnu-Bocquillon, Danielle, *Le mythe de la déesse lointaine à Philae, BdE 132*, (Le Caire/Cairo: IFAO, 2001), 80.

[507] Inconnu-Bocquillon, Danielle, *Le mythe de la déesse lointaine à Philae, BdE 132*, (Le Caire/Cairo: IFAO, 2001), 22.

[508] Leitz, Christian, and Dagmar Budde, et. al. Lexikon der Ägyptischen Götter und Götterbezeichnungen (LGG, OLA 129, Band 8). (Peeters, 2003), 699.

[509] El-Tonssy, Mohamed A. "The Goddess Rattawy in the Greco-Roman Temples" الإلهة رعت تاوى فى معابد العصر اليونانى الرومانى. *The Conference Book of the General Union of Arab Archeologists*. 15. (2012), pp. 195.

[510] Leitz, Christian, and Dagmar Budde, et. al. Lexikon der Ägyptischen Götter und Götterbezeichnungen (LGG, OLA 129, Band 8). (Peeters, 2003), 699.

- Lady of Hibis[511]
- Lady of Kom Ombo[512]
- Lady of the Lesser *Menset* of Heliopolis[513]
- Lady of Light[514]
- Lady of the Lords of Philae[515]
- Lady of the *Per Neser*[516]
- Lady of Per-Netjer (place 5km NW of Esna)[517]
- Lady of Philae[518]
- Lady of Praise[519]
- Lady of the Primordial Time[520]
- Lady of Senmet[521]
- Lady of Splendor[522]
- Lady of Thinis[523]
- Lady of the Two Lands[524]

---

[511] Leitz, Christian, and Dagmar Budde, et. al. Lexikon der Ägyptischen Götter und Götterbezeichnungen (LGG, OLA 129, Band 8). (Peeters, 2003), 699.

[512] Leitz, Christian, and Dagmar Budde, et. al. Lexikon der Ägyptischen Götter und Götterbezeichnungen (LGG, OLA 129, Band 8). (Peeters, 2003), 699.

[513] Leitz, Christian, and Dagmar Budde, et. al. Lexikon der Ägyptischen Götter und Götterbezeichnungen (LGG, OLA 129, Band 8). (Peeters, 2003), 699.

[514] Leitz, Christian, and Dagmar Budde, et. al. Lexikon der Ägyptischen Götter und Götterbezeichnungen (LGG, OLA 129, Band 8). (Peeters, 2003), 698.

[515] Leitz, Christian, and Dagmar Budde, et. al. Lexikon der Ägyptischen Götter und Götterbezeichnungen (LGG, OLA 129, Band 8). (Peeters, 2003), 699.

[516] Leitz, Christian, and Dagmar Budde, et. al. Lexikon der Ägyptischen Götter und Götterbezeichnungen (LGG, OLA 129, Band 8). (Peeters, 2003), 699.

[517] Leitz, Christian, and Dagmar Budde, et. al. Lexikon der Ägyptischen Götter und Götterbezeichnungen (LGG, OLA 129, Band 8). (Peeters, 2003), 699.

[518] Inconnu-Bocquillon, Danielle, *Le mythe de la déesse lointaine à Philae*, BdE 132, (Le Caire/Cairo: IFAO, 2001), 117.

[519] Siuda, Tamara L. The Ancient Egyptian Daybook. (Stargazer Design, 2016), 128. To Hethert-Tefnut/Tefnut-Hethert.

[520] Siuda, Tamara L. The Ancient Egyptian Daybook. (Stargazer Design, 2016), 97.

[521] Inconnu-Bocquillon, Danielle, *Le mythe de la déesse lointaine à Philae*, BdE 132, (Le Caire/Cairo: IFAO, 2001), 23.

[522] Leitz, Christian, and Dagmar Budde, et. al. Lexikon der Ägyptischen Götter und Götterbezeichnungen (LGG, OLA 129, Band 8). (Peeters, 2003), 698.

[523] Leitz, Christian, and Dagmar Budde, et. al. Lexikon der Ägyptischen Götter und Götterbezeichnungen (LGG, OLA 129, Band 8). (Peeters, 2003), 699.

[524] Leitz, Christian, and Dagmar Budde, et. al. Lexikon der Ägyptischen Götter und Götterbezeichnungen (LGG, OLA 129, Band 8). (Peeters, 2003), 699.

- Left Eye[525]
- Life and Ma'at (Shu and Tefnut, respectively)[526]
- Life Snake in the Country[527]
- Lion and Lioness (with Shu)[528]
- Lion of the North[529]
- Lion of the South[530]
- Lioness[531]
- Lioness, Mistress of the Chopping Block, in Eastern Behdet[532]
- Living Daughter[533]
- Lords of the Gods' Things/Offerings/Necropolis[534]
- Lords of Ma'at[535]
- Lords of Power[536]
- Luminous One[537]
- Ma'at[538]

---

[525] De Wit, Constant. *Le rôle et le sens du lion dans l'Égypte ancienne.* (Belgium: E.J. Brill, 1951), 116.

[526] Pinch, Geraldine. Egyptian Mythology: A Guide to the Gods, Goddesses and Traditions of Ancient Egypt. (New York: Oxford University Press, 2004), 64.

[527] Leitz, Christian, and Dagmar Budde, et. al. Lexikon der Ägyptischen Götter und Götterbezeichnungen (LGG, OLA 129, Band 8). (Peeters, 2003), 698.

[528] Sauneron, Serge, *Esna V: Les fêtes religieuses d'Esna aux derniers siècles du paganisme,* (Cairo: IFAO, 1962; 2004), 90. Excerpt from a hymn. Translated by Chelsea Bolton.

[529] Leitz, Christian, and Dagmar Budde, et. al. Lexikon der Ägyptischen Götter und Götterbezeichnungen (LGG, OLA 129, Band 8). (Peeters, 2003), 699.

[530] Leitz, Christian, and Dagmar Budde, et. al. Lexikon der Ägyptischen Götter und Götterbezeichnungen (LGG, OLA 129, Band 8). (Peeters, 2003), 699.

[531] Inconnu-Bocquillon, Danielle, *Le mythe de la déesse lointaine à Philae, BdE 132,* (Le Caire/Cairo: IFAO, 2001), 50.

[532] De Wit, Constant. *Le rôle et le sens du lion dans l'Égypte ancienne.* (Belgium: E.J. Brill, 1951), 331.

[533] Tobin, Vincent Arieh. Theological Principles of Egyptian Religion. Vol. 59. (Lang, Peter, Publishing Incorporated, 1989), 79. Coffin Texts Spell 80.

[534] Leitz, Christian, and Dagmar Budde, et. al. Lexikon der Ägyptischen Götter und Götterbezeichnungen (LGG, OLA 129, Band 8). (Peeters, 2003), 699.

[535] Leitz, Christian, and Dagmar Budde, et. al. Lexikon der Ägyptischen Götter und Götterbezeichnungen (LGG, OLA 129, Band 8). (Peeters, 2003), 700.

[536] Leitz, Christian, and Dagmar Budde, et. al. Lexikon der Ägyptischen Götter und Götterbezeichnungen (LGG, OLA 129, Band 8). (Peeters, 2003), 700.

[537] Leitz, Christian, and Dagmar Budde, et. al. Lexikon der Ägyptischen Götter und Götterbezeichnungen (LGG, OLA 129, Band 8). (Peeters, 2003), 698.

- Mafdet at the Head of Bugem[539]
- Magificent One[540]
- Magnificent or Useful One[541]
- Magnificent and Powerful One[542]
- Makes Her Seat in Senmet in the Company of Her Brother[543]
- Mehit in the House of Mehit (in 8th UE Nome)[544]
- Mighty One in Edfu[545]
- Mistress of All Gods[546]
- Mistress of All the Gods[547]
- Mistress of All the Gods and Goddesses[548]
- Mistress of the Angry Moment[549]
- Mistress of Battle[550]

---

[538] Tobin, Vincent Arieh. Theological Principles of Egyptian Religion. Vol. 59. (Lang, Peter, Publishing Incorporated, 1989), 79. Coffin Texts Spell 80.

[539] De Wit, Constant. *Le rôle et le sens du lion dans l'Égypte ancienne*. (Belgium: E.J. Brill, 1951), 390.

[540] Leitz, Christian, and Dagmar Budde, et. al. Lexikon der Ägyptischen Götter und Götterbezeichnungen (LGG, OLA 129, Band 8). (Peeters, 2003), 702.

[541] Leitz, Christian, and Dagmar Budde, et. al. Lexikon der Ägyptischen Götter und Götterbezeichnungen (LGG, OLA 129, Band 8). (Peeters, 2003), 700.

[542] Leitz, Christian, and Dagmar Budde, et. al. Lexikon der Ägyptischen Götter und Götterbezeichnungen (LGG, OLA 129, Band 8). (Peeters, 2003), 702.

[543] Inconnu-Bocquillon, Danielle, *Le mythe de la déesse lointaine à Philae, BdE 132*, (Le Caire/Cairo: IFAO, 2001), 97.

[544] Leitz, Christian, and Dagmar Budde, et. al. Lexikon der Ägyptischen Götter und Götterbezeichnungen (LGG, OLA 129, Band 8). (Peeters, 2003), 699.

[545] El-Tonssy, Mohamed A. "The Goddess Rattawy in the Greco-Roman Temples" الإلهة رعت تاوى فى معابد العصر اليونانى الرومانى. *The Conference Book of the General Union of Arab Archeologists*. 15. (2012), pp. 195.

[546] El-Tonssy, Mohamed A. "The Goddess Rattawy in the Greco-Roman Temples" الإلهة رعت تاوى فى معابد العصر اليونانى الرومانى. *The Conference Book of the General Union of Arab Archeologists*. 15. (2012), pp. 195.

[547] Preys, René. *Les complexes de la Demeure du Sistre et du Trône de Rê: théologie et décoration dans le temple d'Hathor à Dendera*. Vol. 106. (Peeters Publishers, 2002), 205. El-Tonssy, Mohamed A. "The Goddess Rattawy in the Greco-Roman Temples" الإلهة رعت تاوى فى معابد العصر اليونانى الرومانى. *The Conference Book of the General Union of Arab Archeologists*. 15. (2012), pp. 195.

[548] Leitz, Christian, and Dagmar Budde, et. al. Lexikon der Ägyptischen Götter und Götterbezeichnungen (LGG, OLA 129, Band 8). (Peeters, 2003), 702.

[549] Leitz, Christian, and Dagmar Budde, et. al. Lexikon der Ägyptischen Götter und Götterbezeichnungen (LGG, OLA 129, Band 8). (Peeters, 2003), 702.

- Mistress of Biggeh[551]
- Mistress of the Beginning and End[552]
- Mistress of the Books[553]
- Mistress of the Countries/Lands[554]
- Mistress of Dance[555]
- Mistress of Drunkenness[556]
- Mistress of Embers[557]
- Mistress of Every Sekhmet Goddess[558]
- Mistress of Fear[559]
- Mistress of the Food of Men and Women[560]
- Mistress of the Gods[561]
- Mistress of the Goddesses[562]
- Mistress of the Goddesses of That Name[563]

---

[550] Inconnu-Bocquillon, Danielle, *Le mythe de la déesse lointaine à Philae*, BdE 132, (Le Caire/Cairo: IFAO, 2001), 50.

[551] Hölbl, Günther. Altägypten im Römischen Reich: Die Tempel des römischen Nubien. Vol. 2. (Zabern, 2004), 143.

[552] Leitz, Christian, and Dagmar Budde, et. al. Lexikon der Ägyptischen Götter und Götterbezeichnungen (LGG, OLA 129, Band 8). (Peeters, 2003), 702.

[553] Kaper, Olaf E., and Oe Kaper. The Egyptian God Tutu: a study of the sphinx-god and master of demons with a corpus of monuments. (Peeters Publishers, 2003), 63. Footnote 37.

[554] Leitz, Christian, and Dagmar Budde, et. al. Lexikon der Ägyptischen Götter und Götterbezeichnungen (LGG, OLA 129, Band 8). (Peeters, 2003), 699.

[555] Leitz, Christian, and Dagmar Budde, et. al. Lexikon der Ägyptischen Götter und Götterbezeichnungen (LGG, OLA 129, Band 8). (Peeters, 2003), 701.

[556] Leitz, Christian, and Dagmar Budde, et. al. Lexikon der Ägyptischen Götter und Götterbezeichnungen (LGG, OLA 129, Band 8). (Peeters, 2003), 702.

[557] Spiegelberg, Wilhelm. Der ägyptische Mythus vom Sonnenauge. (Georg Olms Verlag, 1917), 34, footnote 6. This is for Hethert, Tefnut, Bast and Sekhmet.

[558] Leitz, Christian, and Dagmar Budde, et. al. Lexikon der Ägyptischen Götter und Götterbezeichnungen (LGG, OLA 129, Band 8). (Peeters, 2003), 702.

[559] Cauville, Sylvie. Dendara V-VI: II: Index Phraseologique. (Belgium: Peeters, 2004), 519.

[560] Leitz, Christian, and Dagmar Budde, et. al. Lexikon der Ägyptischen Götter und Götterbezeichnungen (LGG, OLA 129, Band 8). (Peeters, 2003), 700.

[561] Leitz, Christian. "Der grosse Repithymnus im Tempel von Athribis." In "Parcourir l'éternité", Hommages à Jean Yoyotte Bd. 2 (Bibliothèque de l'École des Hautes Études, Sciences Religieuses 156), Zivie-Coche, Christiane und Guermeur, Ivan (Hg.), (Turnhout 2012), 759.

[562] Husson, Constance. L'offrande du miroir dans les temples égyptiens de l'époque gréco-romaine. (France: Audin, 1977), 159.

- Mistress of the Greenstone and Papyrus[564]
- Mistress of Heaven[565]
- Mistress of Hermopolis Magna[566]
- Mistress of the House of the Figures/Statues[567]
- Mistress of the House of Wesir[568]
- Mistress of the Human Race[569]
- Mistress of Jewelry[570]
- Mistress of Joy[571]
- Mistress of Jubilation[572]
- Mistress of the Knife Demons[573]
- Mistress of Malachite[574]
- Mistress of the *Menat* of Gold and Faience[575]
- Mistress of Ombos[576]

---

[563] Piehl, Karl. Inscriptions hiéroglyphiques recueillies en Égypte. (Germany: n.p., 1890), 64.

[564] Leitz, Christian, and Dagmar Budde, et. al. Lexikon der Ägyptischen Götter und Götterbezeichnungen (LGG, OLA 129, Band 8). (Peeters, 2003), 700.

[565] Inconnu-Bocquillon, Danielle, *Le mythe de la déesse lointaine à Philae, BdE 132*, (Le Caire/Cairo: IFAO, 2001), 51. Spiegelberg, Wilhelm. *Der ägyptische Mythus vom Sonnenauge*. (Georg Olms Verlag, 1917), 3.

[566] Siuda, Tamara L. The Ancient Egyptian Daybook. (Stargazer Design, 2016), 66.

[567] Leitz, Christian, and Dagmar Budde, et. al. Lexikon der Ägyptischen Götter und Götterbezeichnungen (LGG, OLA 129, Band 8). (Peeters, 2003), 699.

[568] Leitz, Christian, and Dagmar Budde, et. al. Lexikon der Ägyptischen Götter und Götterbezeichnungen (LGG, OLA 129, Band 8). (Peeters, 2003), 699.

[569] Inconnu-Bocquillon, Danielle, *Le mythe de la déesse lointaine à Philae, BdE 132*, (Le Caire/Cairo: IFAO, 2001), 43.

[570] Leitz, Christian, and Dagmar Budde, et. al. Lexikon der Ägyptischen Götter und Götterbezeichnungen (LGG, OLA 129, Band 8). (Peeters, 2003), 700.

[571] Leitz, Christian, and Dagmar Budde, et. al. Lexikon der Ägyptischen Götter und Götterbezeichnungen (LGG, OLA 129, Band 8). (Peeters, 2003), 701.

[572] Leitz, Christian, and Dagmar Budde, et. al. Lexikon der Ägyptischen Götter und Götterbezeichnungen (LGG, OLA 129, Band 8). (Peeters, 2003), 701.

[573] Leitz, Christian, and Dagmar Budde, et. al. Lexikon der Ägyptischen Götter und Götterbezeichnungen (LGG, OLA 129, Band 8). (Peeters, 2003), 702.

[574] Leitz, Christian, and Dagmar Budde, et. al. Lexikon der Ägyptischen Götter und Götterbezeichnungen (LGG, OLA 129, Band 8). (Peeters, 2003), 702.

[575] Leitz, Christian, and Dagmar Budde, et. al. Lexikon der Ägyptischen Götter und Götterbezeichnungen (LGG, OLA 129, Band 8). (Peeters, 2003), 702.

[576] Piehl, Karl. Inscriptions hiéroglyphiques recueillies en Égypte. (Germany: n.p., 1890), 96 and 99.

- Mistress of the Papyrus Pillars[577]
- Mistress of Philae[578]
- Mistress of Pleasure, Joy and Dance[579]
- Mistress of Power[580]
- Mistress of the Red Cloth[581]
- Mistress of the *Sesheshet*-Sistrum[582]
- Mistress of Skinning[583]
- Mistress of the Sky[584]
- Mistress of Terror in the Palace[585]
- Mistress of the Wandering Demons[586]
- Mistress of What the Sun is Orbiting[587]
- Mistress of the Whole Country[588]
- Mistress of Women[589]

[577] Leitz, Christian, and Dagmar Budde, et. al. Lexikon der Ägyptischen Götter und Götterbezeichnungen (LGG, OLA 129, Band 8). (Peeters, 2003), 699.
[578] De Wit, Constant. *Le rôle et le sens du lion dans l'Égypte ancienne.* (Belgium: E.J. Brill, 1951), 330.
[579] Leitz, Christian, and Dagmar Budde, et. al. Lexikon der Ägyptischen Götter und Götterbezeichnungen (LGG, OLA 129, Band 8). (Peeters, 2003), 701.
[580] Leitz, Christian, and Dagmar Budde, et. al. Lexikon der Ägyptischen Götter und Götterbezeichnungen (LGG, OLA 129, Band 8). (Peeters, 2003), 702.
[581] Inconnu-Bocquillon, Danielle, *Le mythe de la déesse lointaine à Philae, BdE 132,* (Le Caire/Cairo: IFAO, 2001), 86.
[582] Leitz, Christian, and Dagmar Budde, et. al. Lexikon der Ägyptischen Götter und Götterbezeichnungen (LGG, OLA 129, Band 8). (Peeters, 2003), 702.
[583] Inconnu-Bocquillon, Danielle, *Le mythe de la déesse lointaine à Philae, BdE 132,* (Le Caire/Cairo: IFAO, 2001), 50.
[584] Inconnu-Bocquillon, Danielle, *Le mythe de la déesse lointaine à Philae, BdE 132,* (Le Caire/Cairo: IFAO, 2001), 101. Piehl, Karl. Inscriptions hiéroglyphiques recueillies en Égypte. (Germany: n.p., 1890), 96.
[585] Leitz, Christian, and Dagmar Budde, et. al. Lexikon der Ägyptischen Götter und Götterbezeichnungen (LGG, OLA 129, Band 8). (Peeters, 2003), 699.
[586] Leitz, Christian, and Dagmar Budde, et. al. Lexikon der Ägyptischen Götter und Götterbezeichnungen (LGG, OLA 129, Band 8). (Peeters, 2003), 702.
[587] Leitz, Christian, and Dagmar Budde, et. al. Lexikon der Ägyptischen Götter und Götterbezeichnungen (LGG, OLA 129, Band 8). (Peeters, 2003), 698.
[588] Leitz, Christian, and Dagmar Budde, et. al. Lexikon der Ägyptischen Götter und Götterbezeichnungen (LGG, OLA 129, Band 8). (Peeters, 2003), 698.
[589] Junker, Hermann. "Der Auszug der Hathor-Tefnut aus Nubien." *Abhandlungen der Preußischen Akademie der Wissenschaften, philosophisch-historische Klasse* (1911), 82. Leitz, Christian, and Dagmar Budde, et. al. Lexikon der Ägyptischen Götter und Götterbezeichnungen (LGG, OLA 129, Band 8). (Peeters, 2003), 702.

- Mistress Who Reads the Festival Scroll[590]
- Mistress of Xois[591]
- My Mistress[592]
- Mother[593]
- Mother of Aset[594]
- Mother of God[595]
- Mother of Mothers[596]
- Mother of Your Mother[597]
- Mother of the Prince of the White Crown[598]
- *Neheh* (Eternal Recurrence) and *Djet* (Eternal Sameness) (Shu and Tefnut)[599]
- Nubian Cat[600]
- Of Vengeance and Revenge[601]
- On the Forehead of Ra[602]

[590] Leitz, Christian, and Dagmar Budde, et. al. Lexikon der Ägyptischen Götter und Götterbezeichnungen (LGG, OLA 129, Band 8). (Peeters, 2003), 702.

[591] Guermeur, Ivan and Christophe Thiers. "Un éloge xoïte de Ptolémée Philadelphe. La stèle BM EA 616". *Bulletin de l'Institut français d'archéologie orientale*, IFAO, 2001), pp.199.

[592] Spiegelberg, Wilhelm. *Der ägyptische Mythus vom Sonnenauge.* (Georg Olms Verlag, 1917), 9.

[593] Inconnu-Bocquillon, Danielle, *Le mythe de la déesse lointaine à Philae*, BdE 132, (Le Caire/Cairo: IFAO, 2001), 23.

[594] Bergman, Jan. Ich Bin Isis: Studien zum memphitischen Hintergrund der griechischen Isisaretalogien. (Almquist & Wiksell, Uppsalla, 1968), 30.
El-Sabban, Sherif. Temple Festival Calendars of Ancient Egypt. (Wiltshire: Liverpool University Press, 2000), 174.

[595] Sauneron, Serge, *Esna V: Les fêtes religieuses d'Esna aux derniers siècles du paganisme,* (Cairo: IFAO, 1962; 2004), 90. Excerpt from a hymn. Translated by Chelsea Bolton.

[596] Leitz, Christian, and Dagmar Budde, et. al. Lexikon der Ägyptischen Götter und Götterbezeichnungen (LGG, OLA 129, Band 8). (Peeters, 2003), 700.

[597] Cauville, Sylvie., Hallof, Jochen., Berg, Hans van den. *Le temple de Dendara: les chapelles osiriennes.* Egypt: (IFAO, 1997), 157.

[598] Leitz, Christian, and Dagmar Budde, et. al. Lexikon der Ägyptischen Götter und Götterbezeichnungen (LGG, OLA 129, Band 8). (Peeters, 2003), 701.

[599] Pinch, Geraldine. Egyptian Mythology: A Guide to the Gods, Goddesses and Traditions of Ancient Egypt. (New York: Oxford University Press, 2004), 197.

[600] Tyldesley, Joyce. The Penguin Book of Myths and Legends of Ancient Egypt. (Penguin Books, 2011), 49.

[601] West, Stephanie. "The Greek version of the legend of Tefnut." *The Journal of Egyptian Archaeology* 55, no. 1 (1969): 178.

- On Whose Head No Other God Overcomes[603]
- One from Kenset[604]
- One from Ta-Sety[605]
- One Who Appears in Philae[606]
- One Who Appears in Senmet[607]
- One Who is Appeased by the Two Lights[608]
- One Who Burns Apep with Her Flame[609]
- One Who Burns the Enemies of Her Father Ra[610]
- One Who Burns with Fire[611]
- One Who Comes from Kenset to Egypt[612]
- One Who Comes from Kenset to Senmet, And Takes Her Seat[613]
- One Who Consumes Apep with the Burning Breath of Her Mouth[614]

---

[602] El-Tonssy, Mohamed A. "The Goddess Rattawy in the Greco-Roman Temples" الإلهة رعت تاوى فى معابد العصر اليونانى الرومانى. *The Conference Book of the General Union of Arab Archeologists. 15.* (2012), pp. 195.

[603] Leitz, Christian, and Dagmar Budde, et. al. <u>Lexikon der Ägyptischen Götter und Götterbezeichnungen (LGG, OLA 129, Band 8).</u> (Peeters, 2003), 700.

[604] Inconnu-Bocquillon, Danielle, *Le mythe de la déesse lointaine à Philae, BdE 132,* (Le Caire/Cairo: IFAO, 2001), 61.

[605] Inconnu-Bocquillon, Danielle, *Le mythe de la déesse lointaine à Philae, BdE 132,* (Le Caire/Cairo: IFAO, 2001), 78.

[606] Inconnu-Bocquillon, Danielle, *Le mythe de la déesse lointaine à Philae, BdE 132,* (Le Caire/Cairo: IFAO, 2001), 86.

[607] Inconnu-Bocquillon, Danielle, *Le mythe de la déesse lointaine à Philae, BdE 132,* (Le Caire/Cairo: IFAO, 2001), 57.

[608] Inconnu-Bocquillon, Danielle, *Le mythe de la déesse lointaine à Philae, BdE 132,* (Le Caire/Cairo: IFAO, 2001), 88.

[609] Inconnu-Bocquillon, Danielle, *Le mythe de la déesse lointaine à Philae, BdE 132,* (Le Caire/Cairo: IFAO, 2001), 83.

[610] Inconnu-Bocquillon, Danielle, *Le mythe de la déesse lointaine à Philae, BdE 132,* (Le Caire/Cairo: IFAO, 2001), 93.

[611] Kockelmann, Holger and Erich Winter, *Philae III: Die Zweite Ostkolonnade des Tempels der Isis in Philae. (CO II und CO II K),* (Verlag der Osterreichischen Akademie der Wissenschaften/Austrian Academy of Sciences, 2016), 189.

[612] Inconnu-Bocquillon, Danielle, *Le mythe de la déesse lointaine à Philae, BdE 132,* (Le Caire/Cairo: IFAO, 2001), 97.

[613] Inconnu-Bocquillon, Danielle, *Le mythe de la déesse lointaine à Philae, BdE 132,* (Le Caire/Cairo: IFAO, 2001), 45.

- One Who Consumes Apep, the Enemy of Her Father Ra[615]
- One Who Consumes the Enemies with the Burning Breath of Her Mouth[616]
- One Who Devours Relative to Her Height[617]
- One Who Dismembers Her Enemies[618]
- One Who Resides in the Castle of the Front[619]
- One Who Resides in Senmet[620]
- One Who is Stable in Elephantine[621]
- One Who Shoots Apep with Her Burning Breath[622]
- One With the Beautiful Face[623]
- One With the Perfect Face[624]
- Perfect One[625]
- Powerful[626]
- Powerful One of the Two Lands[627]

---

[614] Inconnu-Bocquillon, Danielle, *Le mythe de la déesse lointaine à Philae, BdE 132*, (Le Caire/Cairo: IFAO, 2001), 39.

[615] Inconnu-Bocquillon, Danielle, *Le mythe de la déesse lointaine à Philae, BdE 132*, (Le Caire/Cairo: IFAO, 2001), 57.

[616] Inconnu-Bocquillon, Danielle, *Le mythe de la déesse lointaine à Philae, BdE 132*, (Le Caire/Cairo: IFAO, 2001), 43.

[617] Inconnu-Bocquillon, Danielle, *Le mythe de la déesse lointaine à Philae, BdE 132*, (Le Caire/Cairo: IFAO, 2001), 50.

[618] Inconnu-Bocquillon, Danielle, *Le mythe de la déesse lointaine à Philae, BdE 132*, (Le Caire/Cairo: IFAO, 2001), 50.

[619] Inconnu-Bocquillon, Danielle, *Le mythe de la déesse lointaine à Philae, BdE 132*, (Le Caire/Cairo: IFAO, 2001), 88.

[620] Inconnu-Bocquillon, Danielle, *Le mythe de la déesse lointaine à Philae, BdE 132*, (Le Caire/Cairo: IFAO, 2001), 50.

[621] Inconnu-Bocquillon, Danielle, *Le mythe de la déesse lointaine à Philae, BdE 132*, (Le Caire/Cairo: IFAO, 2001), 57.

[622] Inconnu-Bocquillon, Danielle, *Le mythe de la déesse lointaine à Philae, BdE 132*, (Le Caire/Cairo: IFAO, 2001), 87.

[623] Inconnu-Bocquillon, Danielle, *Le mythe de la déesse lointaine à Philae, BdE 132*, (Le Caire/Cairo: IFAO, 2001), 23.

[624] Leitz, Christian, and Dagmar Budde, et. al. <u>Lexikon der Ägyptischen Götter und Götterbezeichnungen (LGG, OLA 129, Band 8).</u> (Peeters, 2003), 700.

[625] Inconnu-Bocquillon, Danielle, *Le mythe de la déesse lointaine à Philae, BdE 132*, (Le Caire/Cairo: IFAO, 2001), 88.

[626] Inconnu-Bocquillon, Danielle, *Le mythe de la déesse lointaine à Philae, BdE 132*, (Le Caire/Cairo: IFAO, 2001), 83.

- Powerful Seshat[628]
- Powerful and Sovereign of the Emisssaries[629]
- Primordial[630]
- Princess of All the Gods[631]
- Protecting Her Son Wesir in Abydos[632]
- Queen of Upper and Lower Egypt[633]
- Radiant Eye of Her Husband[634]
- Regent[635]
- Regent of All the Gods[636]
- Regent of the Goddesses[637]
- Regent and Lady of Philae[638]
- Regent of Philae[639]
- Regent of the Spirits and Emissaries[640]

[627] Leitz, Christian, and Dagmar Budde, et. al. Lexikon der Ägyptischen Götter und Götterbezeichnungen (LGG, OLA 129, Band 8). (Peeters, 2003), 699.

[628] Piehl, Karl. Inscriptions hiéroglyphiques recueillies en Égypte. (Germany: n.p., 1890), 64.

[629] Cauville, Sylvie. Dendara V-VI: II: Index Phraseologique. (Belgium: Peeters, 2004), 518.

[630] De Wit, Constant. Le rôle et le sens du lion dans l'Égypte ancienne. (Belgium: E.J. Brill, 1951), 324.

[631] Hölbl, Günther. Altägypten im Römischen Reich: Die Tempel des römischen Nubien. Vol. 2. (Zabern, 2004), 143.

[632] Leitz, Christian. "Der grosse Repithymnus im Tempel von Athribis." In "Parcourir l'éternité", Hommages à Jean Yoyotte Bd. 2 (Bibliothèque de l'École des Hautes Études, Sciences Religieuses 156), Zivie-Coche, Christiane und Guermeur, Ivan (Hg.), (Turnhout 2012), 759.

[633] Inconnu-Bocquillon, Danielle, Le mythe de la déesse lointaine à Philae, BdE 132, (Le Caire/Cairo: IFAO, 2001), 22.

[634] Leitz, Christian, and Dagmar Budde, et. al. Lexikon der Ägyptischen Götter und Götterbezeichnungen (LGG, OLA 129, Band 8). (Peeters, 2003), 700.

[635] Inconnu-Bocquillon, Danielle, Le mythe de la déesse lointaine à Philae, BdE 132, (Le Caire/Cairo: IFAO, 2001), 43.

[636] Inconnu-Bocquillon, Danielle, Le mythe de la déesse lointaine à Philae, BdE 132, (Le Caire/Cairo: IFAO, 2001), 51. Piehl, Karl. Inscriptions hiéroglyphiques recueillies en Égypte. (Germany: n.p., 1890), 96.

[637] Inconnu-Bocquillon, Danielle, Le mythe de la déesse lointaine à Philae, BdE 132, (Le Caire/Cairo: IFAO, 2001), 92.

[638] Inconnu-Bocquillon, Danielle, Le mythe de la déesse lointaine à Philae, BdE 132, (Le Caire/Cairo: IFAO, 2001), 88.

[639] Inconnu-Bocquillon, Danielle, Le mythe de la déesse lointaine à Philae, BdE 132, (Le Caire/Cairo: IFAO, 2001), 45.

- Regent of the Two Lands[641]
- Resident of Behdet (Edfu)[642]
- Right Eye of Heruakhety[643]
- Right Eye of Ra[644]
- Ruler of Punt[645]
- Ruler of Senmet[646]
- Ruler of the Two Lands[647]
- Ruler of the Two Lands of the Gods[648]
- Secret One[649]
- Sekhmet, the Powerful[650]
- She of the Earth[651]
- She of the Exalted One[652]
- She of the Gold House and the Silver House[653]
- She of Kenset Comes to Biggeh[654]

---

[640] Inconnu-Bocquillon, Danielle, *Le mythe de la déesse lointaine à Philae, BdE 132*, (Le Caire/Cairo: IFAO, 2001), 83.

[641] Inconnu-Bocquillon, Danielle, *Le mythe de la déesse lointaine à Philae, BdE 132*, (Le Caire/Cairo: IFAO, 2001), 22.

[642] De Wit, Constant. *Le rôle et le sens du lion dans l'Égypte ancienne.* (Belgium: E.J. Brill, 1951), 308.

[643] Leitz, Christian, and Dagmar Budde, et. al. <u>Lexikon der Ägyptischen Götter und Götterbezeichnungen (LGG, OLA 129, Band 8).</u> (Peeters, 2003), 700.

[644] Leitz, Christian, and Dagmar Budde, et. al. <u>Lexikon der Ägyptischen Götter und Götterbezeichnungen (LGG, OLA 129, Band 8).</u> (Peeters, 2003), 700.

[645] Leitz, Christian, and Dagmar Budde, et. al. <u>Lexikon der Ägyptischen Götter und Götterbezeichnungen (LGG, OLA 129, Band 8).</u> (Peeters, 2003), 699.

[646] Leitz, Christian, and Dagmar Budde, et. al. <u>Lexikon der Ägyptischen Götter und Götterbezeichnungen (LGG, OLA 129, Band 8).</u> (Peeters, 2003), 699.

[647] Leitz, Christian, and Dagmar Budde, et. al. <u>Lexikon der Ägyptischen Götter und Götterbezeichnungen (LGG, OLA 129, Band 8).</u> (Peeters, 2003), 701.

[648] Leitz, Christian, and Dagmar Budde, et. al. <u>Lexikon der Ägyptischen Götter und Götterbezeichnungen (LGG, OLA 129, Band 8).</u> (Peeters, 2003), 699.

[649] Leitz, Christian, and Dagmar Budde, et. al. <u>Lexikon der Ägyptischen Götter und Götterbezeichnungen (LGG, OLA 129, Band 8).</u> (Peeters, 2003), 702.

[650] Cauville, Sylvie. <u>Dendara V-VI: II: Index Phraseologique.</u> (Belgium: Peeters, 2004), 119.

[651] Leitz, Christian, and Dagmar Budde, et. al. <u>Lexikon der Ägyptischen Götter und Götterbezeichnungen (LGG, OLA 129, Band 8).</u> (Peeters, 2003), 698.

[652] Leitz, Christian, and Dagmar Budde, et. al. <u>Lexikon der Ägyptischen Götter und Götterbezeichnungen (LGG, OLA 129, Band 8).</u> (Peeters, 2003), 702.

[653] Leitz, Christian, and Dagmar Budde, et. al. <u>Lexikon der Ägyptischen Götter und Götterbezeichnungen (LGG, OLA 129, Band 8).</u> (Peeters, 2003), 699.

- She Cleans Her City for Her Son Heru[655]
- She Does Not Depart from You Ever[656]
- She is Angry as Sekhmet and Gracious as Bast[657]
- She is the Eye of Ra[658]
- She is Like the *Menat*[659]
- She Let Out a Piercing Voice[660]
- She Let Out a Piercing Voice with the Power of Her Voice[661]
- She Shook Her Mane[662]
- She Transformed Herself into Her Beautiful Figure of an Angry Lioness[663]
- She Threw Her Husband Away[664]
- She Will Burst Like Flame to the Sky, Then Her Name Will be Sopdet[665]
- She Went to the Palace of Shu at Midday[666]

---

[654] Leitz, Christian, and Dagmar Budde, et. al. Lexikon der Ägyptischen Götter und Götterbezeichnungen (LGG, OLA 129, Band 8). (Peeters, 2003), 698.

[655] Kockelmann, Holger and Erich Winter, *Philae III: Die Zweite Ostkolonnade des Tempels der Isis in Philae. (CO II und CO II K)*, (Verlag der Osterreichischen Akademie der Wissenschaften/Austrian Academy of Sciences, 2016), 263.

[656] Sauneron, Serge, *Esna V: Les fêtes religieuses d'Esna aux derniers siècles du paganisme*, (Cairo: IFAO, 1962; 2004), 90. Excerpt from a hymn. Translated by Chelsea Bolton.

[657] Spiegelberg, Wilhelm. *Der ägyptische Mythus vom Sonnenauge.* (Georg Olms Verlag, 1917), 34, footnote 6. This is for Hethert, Tefnut, Bast and Sekhmet.

[658] Inconnu-Bocquillon, Danielle, *Le mythe de la déesse lointaine à Philae, BdE 132*, (Le Caire/Cairo: IFAO, 2001), 88.

[659] Piehl, Karl. Inscriptions hiéroglyphiques recueillies en Égypte. (Germany: n.p., 1890), 64.

[660] West, Stephanie. "The Greek version of the legend of Tefnut." *The Journal of Egyptian Archaeology* 55, no. 1 (1969): 170.

[661] West, Stephanie. "The Greek version of the legend of Tefnut." *The Journal of Egyptian Archaeology* 55, no. 1 (1969): 170.

[662] Spiegelberg, Wilhelm. *Der ägyptische Mythus vom Sonnenauge.* (Georg Olms Verlag, 1917), 34, footnote 7.

[663] West, Stephanie. "The Greek version of the legend of Tefnut." *The Journal of Egyptian Archaeology* 55, no. 1 (1969): 169.

[664] West, Stephanie. "The Greek version of the legend of Tefnut." *The Journal of Egyptian Archaeology* 55, no. 1 (1969): 169.

[665] Inconnu-Bocquillon, Danielle, *Le mythe de la déesse lointaine à Philae, BdE 132*, (Le Caire/Cairo: IFAO, 2001), 83.

[666] Verhoeven, Ursula. "Eine Vergewaltigung? Vom Umgang mit einer Textstelle des Naos von El Arish (Tefnut-Studien I)." Religion und Philosophie im Alten Ägypten,

- She Who is Above the Upper Ones[667]
- She Who Appears in the Solar Disk[668]
- She Who Brings Apep to a Halt with Her Scorching Breath[669]
- She Who Brings Down Her Enemies[670]
- She Who Burns the Adversaries[671]
- She Who Burns Apep for Her Father Ra[672]
- She Who Burns Apep Through the Scorching Breath of Her Mouth[673]
- She Who Burns Apep with Her Flame[674]
- She Who Burns Enemies[675]
- She Who Burns the Enemies of Her Father Ra[676]
- She Who Burns the Rebels with the Flame from Her Mouth[677]
- She Who Burns the Rebels with Her Scorching Breath[678]
- She Who Burns Set with Her Scorching Breath[679]

Festgabe für Philippe Derchain, Orientalia Lovaniensia Analecta 39, U. Verhoeven, E. Graefe (Hg.), Leuven 1991, 324.

[667] Leitz, Christian, and Dagmar Budde, et. al. Lexikon der Ägyptischen Götter und Götterbezeichnungen (LGG, OLA 129, Band 8). (Peeters, 2003), 702. Thank you to Rev. Tanebet for helping me with this translation.

[668] Leitz, Christian, and Dagmar Budde, et. al. Lexikon der Ägyptischen Götter und Götterbezeichnungen (LGG, OLA 129, Band 8). (Peeters, 2003), 698.

[669] Leitz, Christian, and Dagmar Budde, et. al. Lexikon der Ägyptischen Götter und Götterbezeichnungen (LGG, OLA 129, Band 8). (Peeters, 2003), 700.

[670] Leitz, Christian, and Dagmar Budde, et. al. Lexikon der Ägyptischen Götter und Götterbezeichnungen (LGG, OLA 129, Band 8). (Peeters, 2003), 700.

[671] Leitz, Christian, and Dagmar Budde, et. al. Lexikon der Ägyptischen Götter und Götterbezeichnungen (LGG, OLA 129, Band 8). (Peeters, 2003), 700.

[672] Leitz, Christian, and Dagmar Budde, et. al. Lexikon der Ägyptischen Götter und Götterbezeichnungen (LGG, OLA 129, Band 8). (Peeters, 2003), 700.

[673] Leitz, Christian, and Dagmar Budde, et. al. Lexikon der Ägyptischen Götter und Götterbezeichnungen (LGG, OLA 129, Band 8). (Peeters, 2003), 700.

[674] Leitz, Christian, and Dagmar Budde, et. al. Lexikon der Ägyptischen Götter und Götterbezeichnungen (LGG, OLA 129, Band 8). (Peeters, 2003), 700.

[675] Leitz, Christian, and Dagmar Budde, et. al. Lexikon der Ägyptischen Götter und Götterbezeichnungen (LGG, OLA 129, Band 8). (Peeters, 2003), 700.

[676] Leitz, Christian, and Dagmar Budde, et. al. Lexikon der Ägyptischen Götter und Götterbezeichnungen (LGG, OLA 129, Band 8). (Peeters, 2003), 700.

[677] Leitz, Christian, and Dagmar Budde, et. al. Lexikon der Ägyptischen Götter und Götterbezeichnungen (LGG, OLA 129, Band 8). (Peeters, 2003), 700.

[678] Leitz, Christian, and Dagmar Budde, et. al. Lexikon der Ägyptischen Götter und Götterbezeichnungen (LGG, OLA 129, Band 8). (Peeters, 2003), 700.

- She Who Burns the Wicked with Her Scorching Breath[680]
- She Who Collects the Tributes from the Regions of the Sky[681]
- She Who Comes Out Among the Goddesses[682]
- She Who Comes Out from Bugem (Nubia)[683]
- She Who Comes Out of His (Sun God)'s Body[684]
- She Who Comes from Kenset[685]
- She Who Comes from Kenset to the Eye of Ra (Philae)[686]
- She Who Comes from Nubia[687]
- She Who Comes with Her Brother from Kenset[688]
- She Who Dispels Darkness[689]
- She Who Drives Away the Rebels from the House of the Sistrum[690]
- She Who Embraces Her Father[691]
- She Who Emits the Glow of Her Mouth as a Flame[692]

---

[679] Leitz, Christian, and Dagmar Budde, et. al. Lexikon der Ägyptischen Götter und Götterbezeichnungen (LGG, OLA 129, Band 8). (Peeters, 2003), 700.

[680] Leitz, Christian, and Dagmar Budde, et. al. Lexikon der Ägyptischen Götter und Götterbezeichnungen (LGG, OLA 129, Band 8). (Peeters, 2003), 700.

[681] Leitz, Christian, and Dagmar Budde, et. al. Lexikon der Ägyptischen Götter und Götterbezeichnungen (LGG, OLA 129, Band 8). (Peeters, 2003), 699.

[682] Leitz, Christian, and Dagmar Budde, et. al. Lexikon der Ägyptischen Götter und Götterbezeichnungen (LGG, OLA 129, Band 8). (Peeters, 2003), 701.

[683] Leitz, Christian, and Dagmar Budde, et. al. Lexikon der Ägyptischen Götter und Götterbezeichnungen (LGG, OLA 129, Band 8). (Peeters, 2003), 699.

[684] Leitz, Christian, and Dagmar Budde, et. al. Lexikon der Ägyptischen Götter und Götterbezeichnungen (LGG, OLA 129, Band 8). (Peeters, 2003), 701.

[685] Leitz, Christian, and Dagmar Budde, et. al. Lexikon der Ägyptischen Götter und Götterbezeichnungen (LGG, OLA 129, Band 8). (Peeters, 2003), 699.

[686] Leitz, Christian, and Dagmar Budde, et. al. Lexikon der Ägyptischen Götter und Götterbezeichnungen (LGG, OLA 129, Band 8). (Peeters, 2003), 698.

[687] Leitz, Christian, and Dagmar Budde, et. al. Lexikon der Ägyptischen Götter und Götterbezeichnungen (LGG, OLA 129, Band 8). (Peeters, 2003), 699.

[688] Leitz, Christian, and Dagmar Budde, et. al. Lexikon der Ägyptischen Götter und Götterbezeichnungen (LGG, OLA 129, Band 8). (Peeters, 2003), 699.

[689] Leitz, Christian, and Dagmar Budde, et. al. Lexikon der Ägyptischen Götter und Götterbezeichnungen (LGG, OLA 129, Band 8). (Peeters, 2003), 698.

[690] Leitz, Christian, and Dagmar Budde, et. al. Lexikon der Ägyptischen Götter und Götterbezeichnungen (LGG, OLA 129, Band 8). (Peeters, 2003), 699.

[691] Leitz, Christian, and Dagmar Budde, et. al. Lexikon der Ägyptischen Götter und Götterbezeichnungen (LGG, OLA 129, Band 8). (Peeters, 2003), 701.

- She Who is in His Face[693]
- She Who Fills the Palace with Joy[694]
- She Who Gets to the Body of Her Enemies[695]
- She Who Gives Birth to the Month[696]
- She Who Hears the Homage of Her Brother[697]
- She Who Hides the Secret One, One isn't Supposed to Know[698]
- She Who Keeps the Country Alive Through the Actions of Her Arms[699]
- She Who Lights Up Above the Gods[700]
- She Who Makes All Things Happen[701]
- She Who is Magnificent and Powerful in the House of the Leg[702]
- She Who Lets Everything Which Exists Come into Existence[703]
- She Who is Loved by Her Lord[704]

[692] Leitz, Christian, and Dagmar Budde, et. al. Lexikon der Ägyptischen Götter und Götterbezeichnungen (LGG, OLA 129, Band 8). (Peeters, 2003), 700.

[693] Leitz, Christian, and Dagmar Budde, et. al. Lexikon der Ägyptischen Götter und Götterbezeichnungen (LGG, OLA 129, Band 8). (Peeters, 2003), 702. Thank you to Rev. Tanebet for helping me with this translation.

[694] Leitz, Christian, and Dagmar Budde, et. al. Lexikon der Ägyptischen Götter und Götterbezeichnungen (LGG, OLA 129, Band 8). (Peeters, 2003), 699.

[695] Leitz, Christian, and Dagmar Budde, et. al. Lexikon der Ägyptischen Götter und Götterbezeichnungen (LGG, OLA 129, Band 8). (Peeters, 2003), 700.

[696] Leitz, Christian, and Dagmar Budde, et. al. Lexikon der Ägyptischen Götter und Götterbezeichnungen (LGG, OLA 129, Band 8). (Peeters, 2003), 702.

[697] Leitz, Christian, and Dagmar Budde, et. al. Lexikon der Ägyptischen Götter und Götterbezeichnungen (LGG, OLA 129, Band 8). (Peeters, 2003), 701.

[698] Leitz, Christian, and Dagmar Budde, et. al. Lexikon der Ägyptischen Götter und Götterbezeichnungen (LGG, OLA 129, Band 8). (Peeters, 2003), 701. Thank you to Rev. Tanebet for helping me with this translation.

[699] Leitz, Christian, and Dagmar Budde, et. al. Lexikon der Ägyptischen Götter und Götterbezeichnungen (LGG, OLA 129, Band 8). (Peeters, 2003), 698.

[700] Leitz, Christian, and Dagmar Budde, et. al. Lexikon der Ägyptischen Götter und Götterbezeichnungen (LGG, OLA 129, Band 8). (Peeters, 2003), 698.

[701] Leitz, Christian, and Dagmar Budde, et. al. Lexikon der Ägyptischen Götter und Götterbezeichnungen (LGG, OLA 129, Band 8). (Peeters, 2003), 700.

[702] Leitz, Christian, and Dagmar Budde, et. al. Lexikon der Ägyptischen Götter und Götterbezeichnungen (LGG, OLA 129, Band 8). (Peeters, 2003), 699.

[703] Leitz, Christian, and Dagmar Budde, et. al. Lexikon der Ägyptischen Götter und Götterbezeichnungen (LGG, OLA 129, Band 8). (Peeters, 2003), 700. Thank you to Rev. Tanebet for helping me with this translation.

[704] Siuda, Tamara L. The Ancient Egyptian Daybook. (Stargazer Design, 2016), 286. To Tasenetnofret-Tefnut/Tefnut-Tasenetnofret.

- She Who Loves Ointment[705]
- She Who is the One in Hu[706]
- She Who is from the Swamp of *YrH*[707]
- She Who Places Her Brother on the Throne[708]
- She Who Places Her Brother on the Throne, When She Returns from Asia[709]
- She Who Prepares the Protection of Her Brother in *Pr Wnx*[710]
- She Who Prepares the Protection of the Falcon of the Golden One[711]
- She Who Prepares the Protection of Her Son in the Cities and Nomes[712]
- She Who Prepares the Protection of Her Son Wesir[713]
- She Who Protects Her Brother[714]
- She Who Protects Her Heru Before His Chapel[715]
- She Who Protects the Image of Ihy[716]
- She Who Protects the One Who Created Her[717]

---

[705] Leitz, Christian, and Dagmar Budde, et. al. Lexikon der Ägyptischen Götter und Götterbezeichnungen (LGG, OLA 129, Band 8). (Peeters, 2003), 702.

[706] Leitz, Christian, and Dagmar Budde, et. al. Lexikon der Ägyptischen Götter und Götterbezeichnungen (LGG, OLA 129, Band 8). (Peeters, 2003), 699.

[707] Leitz, Christian, and Dagmar Budde, et. al. Lexikon der Ägyptischen Götter und Götterbezeichnungen (LGG, OLA 129, Band 8). (Peeters, 2003), 699.

[708] Piehl, Karl. Inscriptions hiéroglyphiques recueillies en Égypte. (Germany: n.p., 1890), 99.

[709] Piehl, Karl. Inscriptions hiéroglyphiques recueillies en Égypte. (Germany: n.p., 1890), 99.

[710] Leitz, Christian, and Dagmar Budde, et. al. Lexikon der Ägyptischen Götter und Götterbezeichnungen (LGG, OLA 129, Band 8). (Peeters, 2003), 699.

[711] Leitz, Christian, and Dagmar Budde, et. al. Lexikon der Ägyptischen Götter und Götterbezeichnungen (LGG, OLA 129, Band 8). (Peeters, 2003), 701.

[712] Leitz, Christian, and Dagmar Budde, et. al. Lexikon der Ägyptischen Götter und Götterbezeichnungen (LGG, OLA 129, Band 8). (Peeters, 2003), 699.

[713] Leitz, Christian, and Dagmar Budde, et. al. Lexikon der Ägyptischen Götter und Götterbezeichnungen (LGG, OLA 129, Band 8). (Peeters, 2003), 701.

[714] Leitz, Christian, and Dagmar Budde, et. al. Lexikon der Ägyptischen Götter und Götterbezeichnungen (LGG, OLA 129, Band 8). (Peeters, 2003), 701.

[715] Leitz, Christian, and Dagmar Budde, et. al. Lexikon der Ägyptischen Götter und Götterbezeichnungen (LGG, OLA 129, Band 8). (Peeters, 2003), 699.

[716] Leitz, Christian, and Dagmar Budde, et. al. Lexikon der Ägyptischen Götter und Götterbezeichnungen (LGG, OLA 129, Band 8). (Peeters, 2003), 701.

- She Who Resides in the Abaton[718]
- She Who Resides in Iatdi (Temple of Aset in Dendera)[719]
- She Who Satisfies Her Father[720]
- She Who Satisfies the Two Lands with Her Perfection[721]
- She Who Saves the Property[722]
- She Who Scorches the Mountains with the Glow of Her Mouth[723]
- She Who Sends Out the Fire of Her Majesty Against Her Enemies[724]
- She Who is Thinking...Shore[725]
- She Who is in Akhmim[726]
- She Who is in Coptos[727]
- She Whom Ra Created in the Princely House[728]
- She With Great Popularity in the Heart of Her Father[729]
- She With the Hair Enclosed in a Hairnet[730]

---

[717] Leitz, Christian, and Dagmar Budde, et. al. Lexikon der Ägyptischen Götter und Götterbezeichnungen (LGG, OLA 129, Band 8). (Peeters, 2003), 701.

[718] Leitz, Christian, and Dagmar Budde, et. al. Lexikon der Ägyptischen Götter und Götterbezeichnungen (LGG, OLA 129, Band 8). (Peeters, 2003), 699.

[719] Leitz, Christian, and Dagmar Budde, et. al. Lexikon der Ägyptischen Götter und Götterbezeichnungen (LGG, OLA 129, Band 8). (Peeters, 2003), 699.

[720] Leitz, Christian, and Dagmar Budde, et. al. Lexikon der Ägyptischen Götter und Götterbezeichnungen (LGG, OLA 129, Band 8). (Peeters, 2003), 701.

[721] Leitz, Christian, and Dagmar Budde, et. al. Lexikon der Ägyptischen Götter und Götterbezeichnungen (LGG, OLA 129, Band 8). (Peeters, 2003), 699.

[722] Leitz, Christian, and Dagmar Budde, et. al. Lexikon der Ägyptischen Götter und Götterbezeichnungen (LGG, OLA 129, Band 8). (Peeters, 2003), 701.

[723] Leitz, Christian, and Dagmar Budde, et. al. Lexikon der Ägyptischen Götter und Götterbezeichnungen (LGG, OLA 129, Band 8). (Peeters, 2003), 699.

[724] Leitz, Christian, and Dagmar Budde, et. al. Lexikon der Ägyptischen Götter und Götterbezeichnungen (LGG, OLA 129, Band 8). (Peeters, 2003), 700.

[725] Leitz, Christian, and Dagmar Budde, et. al. Lexikon der Ägyptischen Götter und Götterbezeichnungen (LGG, OLA 129, Band 8). (Peeters, 2003), 699.

[726] Leitz, Christian, and Dagmar Budde, et. al. Lexikon der Ägyptischen Götter und Götterbezeichnungen (LGG, OLA 129, Band 8). (Peeters, 2003), 699.

[727] Leitz, Christian, and Dagmar Budde, et. al. Lexikon der Ägyptischen Götter und Götterbezeichnungen (LGG, OLA 129, Band 8). (Peeters, 2003), 699.

[728] Leitz, Christian, and Dagmar Budde, et. al. Lexikon der Ägyptischen Götter und Götterbezeichnungen (LGG, OLA 129, Band 8). (Peeters, 2003), 699.

[729] Leitz, Christian, and Dagmar Budde, et. al. Lexikon der Ägyptischen Götter und Götterbezeichnungen (LGG, OLA 129, Band 8). (Peeters, 2003), 701.

- She With the Lapis Lazuli Colored Head[731]
- She With the Red Face Against the Enemies of Her Son[732]
- She With the Rough Pupil[733]
- She With a Strong Pair of Arms[734]
- Sister[735]
- Sister of the God Shu[736]
- Sister Next to Her Brother Shu[737]
- Sopdet–Sothis or Sirius[738]
- Souls of Heliopolis (with Ra and Shu)[739]
- Sovereign in Bugem[740]
- Sovereign in Senmet[741]
- Sovereign of All the Gods[742]

---

[730] Leitz, Christian, and Dagmar Budde, et. al. Lexikon der Ägyptischen Götter und Götterbezeichnungen (LGG, OLA 129, Band 8). (Peeters, 2003), 700.

[731] Leitz, Christian, and Dagmar Budde, et. al. Lexikon der Ägyptischen Götter und Götterbezeichnungen (LGG, OLA 129, Band 8). (Peeters, 2003), 700.

[732] Leitz, Christian, and Dagmar Budde, et. al. Lexikon der Ägyptischen Götter und Götterbezeichnungen (LGG, OLA 129, Band 8). (Peeters, 2003), 701.

[733] Leitz, Christian, and Dagmar Budde, et. al. Lexikon der Ägyptischen Götter und Götterbezeichnungen (LGG, OLA 129, Band 8). (Peeters, 2003), 700.

[734] Leitz, Christian, and Dagmar Budde, et. al. Lexikon der Ägyptischen Götter und Götterbezeichnungen (LGG, OLA 129, Band 8). (Peeters, 2003), 700. Thank you to Rev. Tanebet for helping me with this translation.

[735] Siuda, Tamara L. The Ancient Egyptian Daybook. (Stargazer Design, 2016), 60. Tyldesley, Joyce. The Penguin Book of Myths and Legends of Ancient Egypt. (Penguin Books, 2011), 44.

[736] Leitz, Christian, and Dagmar Budde, et. al. Lexikon der Ägyptischen Götter und Götterbezeichnungen (LGG, OLA 129, Band 8). (Peeters, 2003), 701.

[737] Leitz, Christian, and Dagmar Budde, et. al. Lexikon der Ägyptischen Götter und Götterbezeichnungen (LGG, OLA 129, Band 8). (Peeters, 2003), 701.

[738] Inconnu-Bocquillon, Danielle, Le mythe de la déesse lointaine à Philae, BdE 132, (Le Caire/Cairo: IFAO, 2001), 83.

[739] Allen, T. G. The Book of the Dead or Going Forth by Day. (Chicago: University of Chicago Press, 1974), 93. Spell 115.

[740] Richter, Barbara A. "On the Heels of the Wandering Goddess: The Myth and the Festival at the Temples of the Wadi el-Hallel and Dendera." Dolinska, Monika and Beinlich, Horst (eds.) 8. Ägyptologische Tempeltagung: interconnections between temples : Warschau, 22.-25. September 2008. Germany: Harrassowitz, 2010: 167.

[741] Inconnu-Bocquillon, Danielle, Le mythe de la déesse lointaine à Philae, BdE 132, (Le Caire/Cairo: IFAO, 2001), 117.

- Sovereign of the Beloved Country[743]
- Sovereign Among the Goddesses[744]
- Sovereign of the Gods[745]
- Sovereign of Women[746]
- Spiritualize the Dead (wth Shu)[747]
- Sun Goddess[748]
- Sun Goddess in the Two Lands and on the Banks[749]
- Superior of the Place of Execution in Eastern Behdet[750]
- Sweet of Love[751]
- Terrible of Face Against the Enemies of Her Father[752]
- The Body of Her Creator Cannot Be Searched For[753]
- There is No Body of the One Who Created Her[754]
- Twins (with Shu)[755]

[742] De Wit, Constant. *Les Inscriptions du Temple d'Opet a Karnak III: Traduction integrale des textes rituels-Essai d'interpretation.* (Bruxelles : Edition de la Fondation Egyptologique Reine Elisabeth, 1968), 89.

[743] Cauville, Sylvie. Dendara V-VI: II: Index Phraseologique. (Belgium: Peeters, 2004), 506.

[744] Cauville, Sylvie. Dendara II: Traduction. (Belgium: Uitgeverij Peeters, 1999), 183.

[745] De Wit, Constant. *Les Inscriptions du Temple d'Opet a Karnak III: Traduction integrale des textes rituels-Essai d'interpretation.* (Bruxelles : Edition de la Fondation Egyptologique Reine Elisabeth, 1968), 52.

[746] Cauville, Sylvie. "Hathor en tous ses noms," in *BIFAO 115* (2015): 67.

[747] De Wit, Constant. *Le rôle et le sens du lion dans l'Égypte ancienne.* (Belgium: E.J. Brill, 1951), 178.

[748] Leitz, Christian, and Dagmar Budde, et. al. Lexikon der Ägyptischen Götter und Götterbezeichnungen (LGG, OLA 129, Band 8). (Peeters, 2003), 698.

[749] Leitz, Christian, and Dagmar Budde, et. al. Lexikon der Ägyptischen Götter und Götterbezeichnungen (LGG, OLA 129, Band 8). (Peeters, 2003), 698.

[750] Inconnu-Bocquillon, Danielle, *Le mythe de la déesse lointaine à Philae, BdE 132,* (Le Caire/Cairo: IFAO, 2001), 50.

[751] Inconnu-Bocquillon, Danielle, *Le mythe de la déesse lointaine à Philae, BdE 132,* (Le Caire/Cairo: IFAO, 2001), 23.

[752] De Wit, Constant. *Le rôle et le sens du lion dans l'Égypte ancienne.* (Belgium: E.J. Brill, 1951), 329.

[753] Leitz, Christian, and Dagmar Budde, et. al. Lexikon der Ägyptischen Götter und Götterbezeichnungen (LGG, OLA 129, Band 8). (Peeters, 2003), 701. Thank you to Rev. Tanebet for helping me with this translation.

[754] Leitz, Christian, and Dagmar Budde, et. al. Lexikon der Ägyptischen Götter und Götterbezeichnungen (LGG, OLA 129, Band 8). (Peeters, 2003), 700. Thank you to Rev. Tanebet for helping me with this translation.

- Twin Lions of the Horizon (with Shu)[756]
- Twin Souls of Them that are in Mendes (with Shu)[757]
- Two *Bau* (with Shu)[758]
- Two Birds (with Shu)[759]
- Two Birds of Ra (with Shu)[760]
- Two Children (with Shu)[761]
- Two Children of Atum (with Shu)[762]
- Two Children of Ra (with Shu)[763]
- Two Children as Eyes (with Shu)[764]
- Two Crocodiles (with Shu)[765]
- Two Daughters (with Ma'at)[766]
- Two Daughters of the Gods (with Ma'at)[767]
- Two Disks (with Shu)[768]

---

[755] Tyldesley, Joyce. The Penguin Book of Myths and Legends of Ancient Egypt. (Penguin Books, 2011), 43.

[756] Pinch, Geraldine. Egyptian Mythology: A Guide to the Gods, Goddesses and Traditions of Ancient Egypt. (New York: Oxford University Press, 2004), 197.

[757] Allen, T. G. The Book of the Dead or Going Forth by Day. (Chicago: University of Chicago Press, 1974), 29. Spell 17: 14.

[758] Leitz, Christian, and Dagmar Budde, et. al. Lexikon der Ägyptischen Götter und Götterbezeichnungen (LGG, OLA 129, Band 8). (Peeters, 2003), 700.

[759] Sauneron, Serge, Esna V: Les fêtes religieuses d'Esna aux derniers siècles du paganisme, (Cairo: IFAO, 1962; 2004), 90. Excerpt from a hymn. Translated by Chelsea Bolton.

[760] Sauneron, Serge, Esna V: Les fêtes religieuses d'Esna aux derniers siècles du paganisme, (Cairo: IFAO, 1962; 2004), 90. Excerpt from a hymn. Translated by Chelsea Bolton.

[761] Leitz, Christian, and Dagmar Budde, et. al. Lexikon der Ägyptischen Götter und Götterbezeichnungen (LGG, OLA 129, Band 8). (Peeters, 2003), 700.

[762] Sauneron, Serge, Esna V: Les fêtes religieuses d'Esna aux derniers siècles du paganisme, (Cairo: IFAO, 1962; 2004), 90. Excerpt from a hymn. Translated by Chelsea Bolton.

[763] Leitz, Christian, and Dagmar Budde, et. al. Lexikon der Ägyptischen Götter und Götterbezeichnungen (LGG, OLA 129, Band 8). (Peeters, 2003), 700.

[764] Sauneron, Serge, Esna V: Les fêtes religieuses d'Esna aux derniers siècles du paganisme, (Cairo: IFAO, 1962; 2004), 90. Excerpt from a hymn. Leitz, Christian, and Dagmar Budde, et. al. Lexikon der Ägyptischen Götter und Götterbezeichnungen (LGG, OLA 129, Band 8). (Peeters, 2003), 702.

[765] Sternberg-El Hotabi, Heike., Sternberg, Heike. Mythische Motive und Mythenbildung in den ägyptischen Tempeln und Papyri der griechisch-römischen Zeit. (Germany: Harrassowitz, 1985), 38.

[766] Leitz, Christian, and Dagmar Budde, et. al. Lexikon der Ägyptischen Götter und Götterbezeichnungen (LGG, OLA 129, Band 8). (Peeters, 2003), 702.

[767] Leitz, Christian, and Dagmar Budde, et. al. Lexikon der Ägyptischen Götter und Götterbezeichnungen (LGG, OLA 129, Band 8). (Peeters, 2003), 701.

- Two Eyes of Heru (with Shu)[769]
- Two Gods (with Shu)[770]
- Two Great Ones (with Shu)[771]
- Two Great Gods of Heliopolis (with Shu)[772]
- Two Great Spotted Cats (with Shu) [773]
- Two Lions (with Shu)[774]
- Two Powers (with Shu)[775]
- Two Siblings (with Shu)[776]
- Two Who Come Out of Atum (with Shu)[777]
- Under Whose Guidance is the Circumference of the Earth[778]
- Unique Lady[779]
- Unique One[780]
- Upon the Forehead of Ra to Protect His Majesty with Spells[781]

[768] Leitz, Christian, and Dagmar Budde, et. al. Lexikon der Ägyptischen Götter und Götterbezeichnungen (LGG, OLA 129, Band 8). (Peeters, 2003), 698.
[769] Leitz, Christian, and Dagmar Budde, et. al. Lexikon der Ägyptischen Götter und Götterbezeichnungen (LGG, OLA 116, Band 7). (Peeters, 2002), 36-37.
[770] Leitz, Christian, and Dagmar Budde, et. al. Lexikon der Ägyptischen Götter und Götterbezeichnungen (LGG, OLA 129, Band 8). (Peeters, 2003), 702.
[771] Leitz, Christian, and Dagmar Budde, et. al. Lexikon der Ägyptischen Götter und Götterbezeichnungen (LGG, OLA 129, Band 8). (Peeters, 2003), 702. From transliteration of the hieroglyphs.
[772] Leitz, Christian, and Dagmar Budde, et. al. Lexikon der Ägyptischen Götter und Götterbezeichnungen (LGG, OLA 129, Band 8). (Peeters, 2003), 699.
[773] Pinch, Geraldine. Egyptian Mythology: A Guide to the Gods, Goddesses and Traditions of Ancient Egypt. (New York: Oxford University Press, 2004), 197.
[774] Pinch, Geraldine. Egyptian Mythology: A Guide to the Gods, Goddesses and Traditions of Ancient Egypt. (New York: Oxford University Press, 2004), 197.
[775] Leitz, Christian, and Dagmar Budde, et. al. Lexikon der Ägyptischen Götter und Götterbezeichnungen (LGG, OLA 129, Band 8). (Peeters, 2003), 702.
[776] Pinch, Geraldine. Egyptian Mythology: A Guide to the Gods, Goddesses and Traditions of Ancient Egypt. (New York: Oxford University Press, 2004), 63.
[777] Leitz, Christian, and Dagmar Budde, et. al. Lexikon der Ägyptischen Götter und Götterbezeichnungen (LGG, OLA 129, Band 8). (Peeters, 2003), 701.
[778] Leitz, Christian, and Dagmar Budde, et. al. Lexikon der Ägyptischen Götter und Götterbezeichnungen (LGG, OLA 129, Band 8). (Peeters, 2003), 698.
[779] Leitz, Christian, and Dagmar Budde, et. al. Lexikon der Ägyptischen Götter und Götterbezeichnungen (LGG, OLA 129, Band 8). (Peeters, 2003), 702.
[780] Leitz, Christian, and Dagmar Budde, et. al. Lexikon der Ägyptischen Götter und Götterbezeichnungen (LGG, OLA 129, Band 8). (Peeters, 2003), 702.

- *Uraeus*[782]
- *Uraeus* Snake[783]
- *Uraeus* in Bubastis[784]
- *Uraeus* in Her Moment of Fury[785]
- *Uraeus* on the Earth[786]
- *Uraeus* on the Head of the Ennead[787]
- *Uraeus* on the Head of Her Father[788]
- *Uraeus* on His Forehead[789]
- *Uraeus* of Heruakhety[790]
- *Uraeus* of Ra[791]
- *Uraeus* of Her Father[792]
- Uterus That Causes Life in the Womb[793]
- Venerable[794]

---

[781] El-Tonssy, Mohamed A. "The Goddess Rattawy in the Greco-Roman Temples" الإلهة رعت تاوى فى معابد العصر اليونانى الرومانى. *The Conference Book of the General Union of Arab Archeologists*. 15. (2012), pp. 201.

[782] Inconnu-Bocquillon, Danielle, *Le mythe de la déesse lointaine à Philae*, BdE 132, (Le Caire/Cairo: IFAO, 2001), 88.

[783] Kockelmann, Holger and Erich Winter, *Philae III: Die Zweite Ostkolonnade des Tempels der Isis in Philae. (CO II und CO II K)*, (Verlag der Osterreichischen Akademie der Wissenschaften/Austrian Academy of Sciences, 2016), 263.

[784] Cauville, Sylvie. <u>Dendara V-VI: II: Index Phraseologique</u>. (Belgium: Peeters, 2004), 518.

[785] De Wit, Constant. *Les Inscriptions du Temple d'Opet a Karnak III: Traduction integrale des textes rituels-Essai d'interpretation*. (Bruxelles : Edition de la Fondation Egyptologique Reine Elisabeth, 1968), 52.

[786] Leitz, Christian, and Dagmar Budde, et. al. <u>Lexikon der Ägyptischen Götter und Götterbezeichnungen (LGG, OLA 129, Band 8)</u>. (Peeters, 2003), 700.

[787] Leitz, Christian, and Dagmar Budde, et. al. <u>Lexikon der Ägyptischen Götter und Götterbezeichnungen (LGG, OLA 129, Band 8)</u>. (Peeters, 2003), 700.

[788] Leitz, Christian, and Dagmar Budde, et. al. <u>Lexikon der Ägyptischen Götter und Götterbezeichnungen (LGG, OLA 129, Band 8)</u>. (Peeters, 2003), 700.

[789] Inconnu-Bocquillon, Danielle, *Le mythe de la déesse lointaine à Philae*, BdE 132, (Le Caire/Cairo: IFAO, 2001), 23.

[790] Inconnu-Bocquillon, Danielle, *Le mythe de la déesse lointaine à Philae*, BdE 132, (Le Caire/Cairo: IFAO, 2001), 83.

[791] Inconnu-Bocquillon, Danielle, *Le mythe de la déesse lointaine à Philae*, BdE 132, (Le Caire/Cairo: IFAO, 2001), 101.

[792] Leitz, Christian, and Dagmar Budde, et. al. <u>Lexikon der Ägyptischen Götter und Götterbezeichnungen (LGG, OLA 129, Band 8)</u>. (Peeters, 2003), 700.

[793] Leitz, Christian, and Dagmar Budde, et. al. <u>Lexikon der Ägyptischen Götter und Götterbezeichnungen (LGG, OLA 129, Band 8)</u>. (Peeters, 2003), 700.

- Venerable and Excellent[795]
- Venerable and Powerful in the Mound of Tefnut[796]
- Venerable Vulture[797]
- Venerable, Wife of Her Brother Shu[798]
- Very Popular One[799]
- Vulva, Who Gives Birth[800]
- Watcher[801]
- When She Comes from Bugem (Nubia)[802]
- While She is Angry[803]
- Who Appears with the Solar Disk[804]
- Who is Appeased by the Glorification of the Two Sistra[805]
- Who Are in Heliopolis (with Shu and Atum)[806]
- Who Attends Senmet in the Form of the Venerable Wepeset[807]
- Who is in Atum[808]

---

[794] Inconnu-Bocquillon, Danielle, *Le mythe de la déesse lointaine à Philae, BdE 132*, (Le Caire/Cairo: IFAO, 2001), 43.

[795] Cauville, Sylvie. Dendara II: Traduction. (Belgium: Uitgeverij Peeters, 1999), 183.

[796] Cauville, Sylvie., Lecler, Alain. Dendara I: Traduction. (Belgium: Peeters, 1998), 79.

[797] Leitz, Christian, and Dagmar Budde, et. al. Lexikon der Ägyptischen Götter und Götterbezeichnungen (LGG, OLA 129, Band 8). (Peeters, 2003), 700.

[798] Inconnu-Bocquillon, Danielle, *Le mythe de la déesse lointaine à Philae, BdE 132*, (Le Caire/Cairo: IFAO, 2001), 39.

[799] Leitz, Christian, and Dagmar Budde, et. al. Lexikon der Ägyptischen Götter und Götterbezeichnungen (LGG, OLA 129, Band 8). (Peeters, 2003), 701. Thank you to Rev. Tanebetheru for her help with this translation.

[800] Leitz, Christian, and Dagmar Budde, et. al. Lexikon der Ägyptischen Götter und Götterbezeichnungen (LGG, OLA 129, Band 8). (Peeters, 2003), 700.

[801] Leitz, Christian, and Dagmar Budde, et. al. Lexikon der Ägyptischen Götter und Götterbezeichnungen (LGG, OLA 129, Band 8). (Peeters, 2003), 702.

[802] Inconnu-Bocquillon, Danielle, *Le mythe de la déesse lointaine à Philae, BdE 132*, (Le Caire/Cairo: IFAO, 2001), 78.

[803] Inconnu-Bocquillon, Danielle, *Le mythe de la déesse lointaine à Philae, BdE 132*, (Le Caire/Cairo: IFAO, 2001), 78.

[804] Cauville, Sylvie. Dendara V-VI: II: Index Phraseologique. (Belgium: Peeters, 2004), 519.

[805] Inconnu-Bocquillon, Danielle, *Le mythe de la déesse lointaine à Philae, BdE 132*, (Le Caire/Cairo: IFAO, 2001), 86.

[806] Allen, T. G. *The Book of the Dead or Going Forth by Day*. (Chicago: University of Chicago Press, 1974), 200. Spell 182: d.

[807] Inconnu-Bocquillon, Danielle, *Le mythe de la déesse lointaine à Philae, BdE 132*, (Le Caire/Cairo: IFAO, 2001), 22.

- Who Belongs to the Head of Her Father[809]
- Who Burns Her Enemies[810]
- Who Burns Her Father's Enemies[811]
- Who Burns the Enemies with Her Breath[812]
- Who Conceals Her Body from Her Ancestors[813]
- Who Created Your Beauty (with Shu and Atum)[814]
- Who Does Not Stray from Him (Shu) to Any Other Place[815]
- Who Embraces Her Brother[816]
- Who Embraces Shu in the Leg Room[817]
- Who Gave Birth to Her Father[818]
- Who Gave Birth to the Gods[819]
- Who Gives Birth to the Ennead[820]
- Who Gives Birth to the Gods[821]
- Who Fills the Heart of Ra with Joy[822]

---

[808] Leitz, Christian, and Dagmar Budde, et. al. Lexikon der Ägyptischen Götter und Götterbezeichnungen (LGG, OLA 129, Band 8). (Peeters, 2003), 702.

[809] Leitz, Christian, and Dagmar Budde, et. al. Lexikon der Ägyptischen Götter und Götterbezeichnungen (LGG, OLA 129, Band 8). (Peeters, 2003), 700.

[810] Inconnu-Bocquillon, Danielle, Le mythe de la déesse lointaine à Philae, BdE 132, (Le Caire/Cairo: IFAO, 2001), 88.

[811] Inconnu-Bocquillon, Danielle, Le mythe de la déesse lointaine à Philae, BdE 132, (Le Caire/Cairo: IFAO, 2001), 86.

[812] Cauville, Sylvie. Dendara II: Traduction. (Belgium: Uitgeverij Peeters, 1999), 713.

[813] Leitz, Christian, and Dagmar Budde, et. al. Lexikon der Ägyptischen Götter und Götterbezeichnungen (LGG, OLA 129, Band 8). (Peeters, 2003), 702.

[814] Allen, T. G. The Book of the Dead or Going Forth by Day. (Chicago: University of Chicago Press, 1974), 200. Spell 182: d. I changed "thy" to "your".

[815] Inconnu-Bocquillon, Danielle, Le mythe de la déesse lointaine à Philae, BdE 132, (Le Caire/Cairo: IFAO, 2001), 39.

[816] De Wit, Constant. Le rôle et le sens du lion dans l'Égypte ancienne. (Belgium: E.J. Brill, 1951), 329.

[817] De Wit, Constant. Le rôle et le sens du lion dans l'Égypte ancienne. (Belgium: E.J. Brill, 1951), 308.

[818] Siuda, Tamara L. The Ancient Egyptian Daybook. (Stargazer Design, 2016), 59.

[819] De Wit, Constant. Les Inscriptions du Temple d'Opet a Karnak III: Traduction integrale des textes rituels-Essai d'interpretation. (Bruxelles : Edition de la Fondation Egyptologique Reine Elisabeth, 1968), 89.

[820] Goyon, Jean-Claude. "Inscriptions Tardives Du Temple De Mout à Karnak." Journal of the American Research Center in Egypt 20 (1983): 56-57. Mut-Tefnut-Aset.

[821] Inconnu-Bocquillon, Danielle, Le mythe de la déesse lointaine à Philae, BdE 132, (Le Caire/Cairo: IFAO, 2001), 23.

- Who Fulfills Her Brother's Wish[823]
- Who Flies Against the Enemies of Her Son[824]
- Who is at the Head of Philae[825]
- Who Ignites the Two Hills With the Burning Breath from Her Mouth[826]
- Who Illuminates the Two Lands[827]
- Who Lives in the Palace of the Hawk[828]
- Who Loves Brightness[829]
- Who Makes the Protection of the Golden Falcon[830]
- Who Made the Gods, Who Begot the Gods and Established the Gods (wth Shu)[831]
- Who Offers the Breath of Life to Her Father[832]
- Who Overthrows Her Enemy[833]
- Who Overthrows His Enemies (of Her Father) in His City of Edfu[834]

---

[822] Cauville, Sylvie., Lecler, Alain. Dendara I: Traduction. (Belgium: Peeters, 1998), 79.

[823] Leitz, Christian. "Der grosse Repithymnus im Tempel von Athribis." In "Parcourir l'éternité", Hommages à Jean Yoyotte Bd. 2 (Bibliothèque de l'École des Hautes Études, Sciences Religieuses 156), Zivie-Coche, Christiane und Guermeur, Ivan (Hg.), (Turnhout 2012), 766.

[824] Inconnu-Bocquillon, Danielle, *Le mythe de la déesse lointaine à Philae*, BdE 132, (Le Caire/Cairo: IFAO, 2001), 50.

[825] Inconnu-Bocquillon, Danielle, *Le mythe de la déesse lointaine à Philae*, BdE 132, (Le Caire/Cairo: IFAO, 2001), 86.

[826] Inconnu-Bocquillon, Danielle, *Le mythe de la déesse lointaine à Philae*, BdE 132, (Le Caire/Cairo: IFAO, 2001), 80.

[827] Inconnu-Bocquillon, Danielle, *Le mythe de la déesse lointaine à Philae*, BdE 132, (Le Caire/Cairo: IFAO, 2001), 88.

[828] Piehl, Karl. Inscriptions hiéroglyphiques recueillies en Égypte. (Germany: n.p., 1890), 99.

[829] Inconnu-Bocquillon, Danielle, *Le mythe de la déesse lointaine à Philae*, BdE 132, (Le Caire/Cairo: IFAO, 2001), 86.

[830] Cauville, Sylvie. Dendara V-VI: II: Index Phraseologique. (Belgium: Peeters, 2004), 519.

[831] Faulkner, Raymond O. The Ancient Egyptian Pyramid Texts. (London: Oxford University Press, 1969), 90. PT 301.

[832] Piehl, Karl. Inscriptions hiéroglyphiques recueillies en Égypte. (Germany: n.p., 1890), 11.

[833] Cauville, Sylvie. Dendara V-VI: II: Index Phraseologique. (Belgium: Peeters, 2004), 519.

[834] De Wit, Constant. *Le rôle et le sens du lion dans l'Égypte ancienne*. (Belgium: E.J. Brill, 1951), 329.

- Who Protects His Majesty Daily[835]
- Who Protects His Majesty Daily and Unites with Him in Senmet[836]
- Who Puts Your Victory Against Your Enemies[837]
- Who Reaches the Members of Her Adversaries[838]
- Who Resides in Abaton[839]
- Who Resides in Biggeh[840]
- Who Resides in Iatdi[841]
- Who Resides in Senmet[842]
- Who Scorches the Mountains with Her Flame[843]
- Who Sends Out the Messengers at the End of the Year[844]
- Who Sends Out the *hbiw* Demons of the End of the Year[845]
- Who Spits Her Majesty's Flame Against the Rebels[846]
- Who Slaughters the Enemies of the House of the Sistrum[847]

---

[835] Inconnu-Bocquillon, Danielle, *Le mythe de la déesse lointaine à Philae, BdE 132*, (Le Caire/Cairo: IFAO, 2001), 93.

[836] Inconnu-Bocquillon, Danielle, *Le mythe de la déesse lointaine à Philae, BdE 132*, (Le Caire/Cairo: IFAO, 2001), 93.

[837] Gaber, Amr. "The Central Hall in the Egyptian Temples of the Ptolemaic Period." (PhD diss., Durham University, 2009), 402.

[838] Preys, René. *Les complexes de la Demeure du Sistre et du Trône de Rê: théologie et décoration dans le temple d'Hathor à Dendera*. Vol. 106. (Peeters Publishers, 2002), 205.

[839] Inconnu-Bocquillon, Danielle, *Le mythe de la déesse lointaine à Philae, BdE 132*, (Le Caire/Cairo: IFAO, 2001), 45. Gaber, Amr. "The Central Hall in the Egyptian Temples of the Ptolemaic Period." (PhD diss., Durham University, 2009), 97-98.

[840] Gaber, Amr. "The Central Hall in the Egyptian Temples of the Ptolemaic Period." (PhD diss., Durham University, 2009), 97.

[841] Preys, René. *Les complexes de la Demeure du Sistre et du Trône de Rê: théologie et décoration dans le temple d'Hathor à Dendera*. Vol. 106. (Peeters Publishers, 2002), 205.

[842] Inconnu-Bocquillon, Danielle, *Le mythe de la déesse lointaine à Philae, BdE 132*, (Le Caire/Cairo: IFAO, 2001), 22.

[843] Spiegelberg, Wilhelm. *Der ägyptische Mythus vom Sonnenauge.* (Georg Olms Verlag, 1917), 34, footnote 6. This is for Hethert, Tefnut, Bast and Sekhmet.

[844] Leitz, Christian, and Dagmar Budde, et. al. Lexikon der Ägyptischen Götter und Götterbezeichnungen (LGG, OLA 129, Band 8). (Peeters, 2003), 702.

[845] Kaper, Olaf E., and Oe Kaper. The Egyptian God Tutu: a study of the sphinx-god and master of demons with a corpus of monuments. (Peeters Publishers, 2003), 63. Footnote 37.

[846] Cauville, Sylvie. Dendara V-VI: II: Index Phraseologique. (Belgium: Peeters, 2004), 518.

[847] Preys, René. *Les complexes de la Demeure du Sistre et du Trône de Rê: théologie et décoration dans le temple d'Hathor à Dendera*. Vol. 106. (Peeters Publishers, 2002), 205.

- Who Springs from Kenset[848]
- Who Yourselves Created Your Godheads and Your Persons (with Shu)[849]
- Whose Body is Youthful as the Two Children of Ra (with Shu)[850]
- Whose Flame is Great Against Set[851]
- Whose Heart Rejoices When He (Ra) Sees Her[852]
- Whose Love is Sweet[853]
- Whose Plans are Hidden in El-Tod[854]
- Whose Pupil is Frightful[855]
- Wife of Her Brother Shu[856]
- Wife of God[857]
- Whispering Cat[858]
- White One[859]
- With the Beautiful Face[860]

[848] Inconnu-Bocquillon, Danielle, *Le mythe de la déesse lointaine à Philae, BdE 132*, (Le Caire/Cairo: IFAO, 2001), 22.

[849] Faulkner, Raymond O. The Ancient Egyptian Pyramid Texts. (London: Oxford University Press, 1969), 90. PT 301.

[850] Leitz, Christian, and Dagmar Budde, et. al. Lexikon der Ägyptischen Götter und Götterbezeichnungen (LGG, OLA 129, Band 8). (Peeters, 2003), 700.

[851] Preys, René. *Les complexes de la Demeure du Sistre et du Trône de Rê: théologie et décoration dans le temple d'Hathor à Dendera*. Vol. 106. (Peeters Publishers, 2002), 205.

[852] Inconnu-Bocquillon, Danielle, *Le mythe de la déesse lointaine à Philae, BdE 132*, (Le Caire/Cairo: IFAO, 2001), 57.

[853] Cauville, Sylvie. Dendara II: Traduction. (Belgium: Uitgeverij Peeters, 1999), 183.

[854] El-Tonssy, Mohamed A. "The Goddess Rattawy in the Greco-Roman Temples" الإلهة رعت تاوى فى معابد العصر اليونانى الرومانى. *The Conference Book of the General Union of Arab Archeologists*. 15. (2012), pp. 195.

[855] Piehl, Karl. Inscriptions hiéroglyphiques recueillies en Égypte. (Germany: n.p., 1890), 64.

[856] Inconnu-Bocquillon, Danielle, *Le mythe de la déesse lointaine à Philae, BdE 132*, (Le Caire/Cairo: IFAO, 2001), 39.

[857] Leitz, Christian, and Dagmar Budde, et. al. Lexikon der Ägyptischen Götter und Götterbezeichnungen (LGG, OLA 129, Band 8). (Peeters, 2003), 701.

[858] West, Stephanie. "The Greek version of the legend of Tefnut." *The Journal of Egyptian Archaeology* 55, no. 1 (1969): 178.

[859] Leitz, Christian, and Dagmar Budde, et. al. Lexikon der Ägyptischen Götter und Götterbezeichnungen (LGG, OLA 129, Band 8). (Peeters, 2003), 700.

- With Great Heat[861]
- With the Head of Lapis[862]
- With Her Daughter Nut[863]
- With Many Cobras (a Crown)[864]
- With Painful Fury[865]
- With the Secret Image[866]
- With the Shiny Face[867]
- With a Red Face Against Her Son's Enemy[868]
- Without Her Likeness[869]
- Yesterday and Tomorrow (with Shu)[870]
- You are Called the Whispering Cat, Because it is She Who Whispers in the Ear of the Earthlings[871]
- You are the Member of Vengeance and Revenge, Namely the Daughter of Ra[872]

---

[860] Inconnu-Bocquillon, Danielle, Le mythe de la déesse lointaine à Philae, BdE 132, (Le Caire/Cairo: IFAO, 2001), 23. Cauville, Sylvie. Dendara II: Traduction. (Belgium: Uitgeverij Peeters, 1999), 183.

[861] Leitz, Christian, and Dagmar Budde, et. al. Lexikon der Ägyptischen Götter und Götterbezeichnungen (LGG, OLA 129, Band 8). (Peeters, 2003), 702.

[862] Husson, Constance. L'offrande du miroir dans les temples égyptiens de l'époque gréco-romaine. (France: Audin, 1977), 159.

[863] Junker, Hermann. "Der Auszug der Hathor-Tefnut aus Nubien." Abhandlungen der Preußischen Akademie der Wissenschaften, philosophisch-historische Klasse (1911), 60.

[864] Leitz, Christian, and Dagmar Budde, et. al. Lexikon der Ägyptischen Götter und Götterbezeichnungen (LGG, OLA 129, Band 8). (Peeters, 2003), 701.

[865] Leitz, Christian, and Dagmar Budde, et. al. Lexikon der Ägyptischen Götter und Götterbezeichnungen (LGG, OLA 129, Band 8). (Peeters, 2003), 702.

[866] Leitz, Christian, and Dagmar Budde, et. al. Lexikon der Ägyptischen Götter und Götterbezeichnungen (LGG, OLA 129, Band 8). (Peeters, 2003), 702.

[867] Leitz, Christian, and Dagmar Budde, et. al. Lexikon der Ägyptischen Götter und Götterbezeichnungen (LGG, OLA 129, Band 8). (Peeters, 2003), 700.

[868] Junker, Hermann. "Der Auszug der Hathor-Tefnut aus Nubien." Abhandlungen der Preußischen Akademie der Wissenschaften, philosophisch-historische Klasse (1911), 36.

[869] Leitz, Christian, and Dagmar Budde, et. al. Lexikon der Ägyptischen Götter und Götterbezeichnungen (LGG, OLA 129, Band 8). (Peeters, 2003), 702.

[870] Pinch, Geraldine. Egyptian Mythology: A Guide to the Gods, Goddesses and Traditions of Ancient Egypt. (New York: Oxford University Press, 2004), 197.

[871] West, Stephanie. "The Greek version of the legend of Tefnut." The Journal of Egyptian Archaeology 55, no. 1 (1969): 178.

[872] West, Stephanie. "The Greek version of the legend of Tefnut." The Journal of Egyptian Archaeology 55, no. 1 (1969): 178.

- You Do What She Has Commanded[873]
- You Do Not Turn Away from What She Says[874]
- Your Mother Tefnut is Your Protection[875]

[873] Leitz, Christian, and Dagmar Budde, et. al. <u>Lexikon der Ägyptischen Götter und Götterbezeichnungen (LGG, OLA 129, Band 8).</u> (Peeters, 2003), 701.

[874] Leitz, Christian, and Dagmar Budde, et. al. <u>Lexikon der Ägyptischen Götter und Götterbezeichnungen (LGG, OLA 129, Band 8).</u> (Peeters, 2003), 701.

[875] De Wit, Constant. *Le rôle et le sens du lion dans l'Égypte ancienne.* (Belgium: E.J. Brill, 1951), 332.

Titles of Tefnut-Tasenetnofret

- At Whose Sight Everyone Lives[876]
- Beautiful Sister at the Side of Her Brother[877]
- Beloved of Her Lord[878]
- Bright One[879]
- Cobra of Her Father[880]
- Excellent Maiden[881]
- Eye of Ra[882]
- Eye of Ra in the Circuit of the Sun Disk[883]
- Female Ra in the World/Raet in the World[884]
- Foremost of the Horizon[885]
- Foremost of the House of the Falcon[886]
- Foremost of the House of the Figures/Statues[887]

[876] Leitz, Christian, and Dagmar Budde, et. al. Lexikon der Ägyptischen Götter und Götterbezeichnungen (LGG, OLA 129, Band 8). (Peeters, 2003), 694.
[877] Leitz, Christian, and Dagmar Budde, et. al. Lexikon der Ägyptischen Götter und Götterbezeichnungen (LGG, OLA 129, Band 8). (Peeters, 2003), 694.
[878] Leitz, Christian, and Dagmar Budde, et. al. Lexikon der Ägyptischen Götter und Götterbezeichnungen (LGG, OLA 129, Band 8). (Peeters, 2003), 694.
[879] Leitz, Christian, and Dagmar Budde, et. al. Lexikon der Ägyptischen Götter und Götterbezeichnungen (LGG, OLA 129, Band 8). (Peeters, 2003), 693.
[880] Leitz, Christian, and Dagmar Budde, et. al. Lexikon der Ägyptischen Götter und Götterbezeichnungen (LGG, OLA 129, Band 8). (Peeters, 2003), 694.
[881] Leitz, Christian, and Dagmar Budde, et. al. Lexikon der Ägyptischen Götter und Götterbezeichnungen (LGG, OLA 129, Band 8). (Peeters, 2003), 694.
[882] Leitz, Christian, and Dagmar Budde, et. al. Lexikon der Ägyptischen Götter und Götterbezeichnungen (LGG, OLA 129, Band 8). (Peeters, 2003), 694.
[883] Leitz, Christian, and Dagmar Budde, et. al. Lexikon der Ägyptischen Götter und Götterbezeichnungen (LGG, OLA 129, Band 8). (Peeters, 2003), 693.
[884] Leitz, Christian, and Dagmar Budde, et. al. Lexikon der Ägyptischen Götter und Götterbezeichnungen (LGG, OLA 129, Band 8). (Peeters, 2003), 693.
[885] Leitz, Christian, and Dagmar Budde, et. al. Lexikon der Ägyptischen Götter und Götterbezeichnungen (LGG, OLA 129, Band 8). (Peeters, 2003), 693.
[886] Leitz, Christian, and Dagmar Budde, et. al. Lexikon der Ägyptischen Götter und Götterbezeichnungen (LGG, OLA 129, Band 8). (Peeters, 2003), 694.

- Foremost of the King's House[888]
- Golden One[889]
- Great[890]
- Great Burning One[891]
- Great Cobra on the Head of Ra[892]
- Great *Djedet* of the Nine Bows (Foreigners)[893]
- Great Flame[894]
- Great Mistress of Upper and Lower Egypt[895]
- Great One Who Hears[896]
- Lady of Love[897]
- Lady of the Palace[898]
- Living Cobra of the King in His Day[899]
- Magnificent One[900]

---

[887] Leitz, Christian, and Dagmar Budde, et. al. Lexikon der Ägyptischen Götter und Götterbezeichnungen (LGG, OLA 129, Band 8). (Peeters, 2003), 694.

[888] Leitz, Christian, and Dagmar Budde, et. al. Lexikon der Ägyptischen Götter und Götterbezeichnungen (LGG, OLA 129, Band 8). (Peeters, 2003), 694.

[889] Leitz, Christian, and Dagmar Budde, et. al. Lexikon der Ägyptischen Götter und Götterbezeichnungen (LGG, OLA 129, Band 8). (Peeters, 2003), 694.

[890] Leitz, Christian, and Dagmar Budde, et. al. Lexikon der Ägyptischen Götter und Götterbezeichnungen (LGG, OLA 129, Band 8). (Peeters, 2003), 694.

[891] Leitz, Christian, and Dagmar Budde, et. al. Lexikon der Ägyptischen Götter und Götterbezeichnungen (LGG, OLA 129, Band 8). (Peeters, 2003), 694.

[892] Leitz, Christian, and Dagmar Budde, et. al. Lexikon der Ägyptischen Götter und Götterbezeichnungen (LGG, OLA 129, Band 8). (Peeters, 2003), 694.

[893] Leitz, Christian, and Dagmar Budde, et. al. Lexikon der Ägyptischen Götter und Götterbezeichnungen (LGG, OLA 129, Band 8). (Peeters, 2003), 693.

[894] Leitz, Christian, and Dagmar Budde, et. al. Lexikon der Ägyptischen Götter und Götterbezeichnungen (LGG, OLA 129, Band 8). (Peeters, 2003), 694.

[895] Leitz, Christian, and Dagmar Budde, et. al. Lexikon der Ägyptischen Götter und Götterbezeichnungen (LGG, OLA 129, Band 8). (Peeters, 2003), 693.

[896] Leitz, Christian, and Dagmar Budde, et. al. Lexikon der Ägyptischen Götter und Götterbezeichnungen (LGG, OLA 129, Band 8). (Peeters, 2003), 694.

[897] Leitz, Christian, and Dagmar Budde, et. al. Lexikon der Ägyptischen Götter und Götterbezeichnungen (LGG, OLA 129, Band 8). (Peeters, 2003), 694.

[898] Leitz, Christian, and Dagmar Budde, et. al. Lexikon der Ägyptischen Götter und Götterbezeichnungen (LGG, OLA 129, Band 8). (Peeters, 2003), 694.

[899] Leitz, Christian, and Dagmar Budde, et. al. Lexikon der Ägyptischen Götter und Götterbezeichnungen (LGG, OLA 129, Band 8). (Peeters, 2003), 694.

[900] Leitz, Christian, and Dagmar Budde, et. al. Lexikon der Ägyptischen Götter und Götterbezeichnungen (LGG, OLA 129, Band 8). (Peeters, 2003), 694.

- Magnificent and Powerful[901]
- Magnificent on Earth[902]
- Mistress[903]
- Mistress of All the Gods[904]
- Mistress of Drunkenness[905]
- Mistress of Food[906]
- Mistress of the Gods[907]
- Mistress of the Gods and Goddesses[908]
- Mistress of Goddesses[909]
- Mistress of the House of Flame[910]
- Mistress of the King's House[911]
- Mistress of Kom Ombo[912]
- Mistress of Life[913]
- Mistress of Men and Women[914]

[901] Leitz, Christian, and Dagmar Budde, et. al. Lexikon der Ägyptischen Götter und Götterbezeichnungen (LGG, OLA 129, Band 8). (Peeters, 2003), 694.

[902] Leitz, Christian, and Dagmar Budde, et. al. Lexikon der Ägyptischen Götter und Götterbezeichnungen (LGG, OLA 129, Band 8). (Peeters, 2003), 693.

[903] Leitz, Christian, and Dagmar Budde, et. al. Lexikon der Ägyptischen Götter und Götterbezeichnungen (LGG, OLA 129, Band 8). (Peeters, 2003), 694.

[904] Leitz, Christian, and Dagmar Budde, et. al. Lexikon der Ägyptischen Götter und Götterbezeichnungen (LGG, OLA 129, Band 8). (Peeters, 2003), 694.

[905] Leitz, Christian, and Dagmar Budde, et. al. Lexikon der Ägyptischen Götter und Götterbezeichnungen (LGG, OLA 129, Band 8). (Peeters, 2003), 695.

[906] Leitz, Christian, and Dagmar Budde, et. al. Lexikon der Ägyptischen Götter und Götterbezeichnungen (LGG, OLA 129, Band 8). (Peeters, 2003), 695.

[907] Leitz, Christian, and Dagmar Budde, et. al. Lexikon der Ägyptischen Götter und Götterbezeichnungen (LGG, OLA 129, Band 8). (Peeters, 2003), 694.

[908] Leitz, Christian, and Dagmar Budde, et. al. Lexikon der Ägyptischen Götter und Götterbezeichnungen (LGG, OLA 129, Band 8). (Peeters, 2003), 694.

[909] Leitz, Christian, and Dagmar Budde, et. al. Lexikon der Ägyptischen Götter und Götterbezeichnungen (LGG, OLA 129, Band 8). (Peeters, 2003), 694.

[910] Leitz, Christian, and Dagmar Budde, et. al. Lexikon der Ägyptischen Götter und Götterbezeichnungen (LGG, OLA 129, Band 8). (Peeters, 2003), 694.

[911] Leitz, Christian, and Dagmar Budde, et. al. Lexikon der Ägyptischen Götter und Götterbezeichnungen (LGG, OLA 129, Band 8). (Peeters, 2003), 694.

[912] Leitz, Christian, and Dagmar Budde, et. al. Lexikon der Ägyptischen Götter und Götterbezeichnungen (LGG, OLA 129, Band 8). (Peeters, 2003), 693.

[913] Leitz, Christian, and Dagmar Budde, et. al. Lexikon der Ägyptischen Götter und Götterbezeichnungen (LGG, OLA 129, Band 8). (Peeters, 2003), 694.

- Mistress of the Papyurs Pillars[915]
- Mistress of Women[916]
- Most Beautiful on the Head of Her Father Ra[917]
- Perfect and Magnificent One[918]
- Power is Great Against the Enemies of Her Father[919]
- Powerful in the Sky[920]
- Richly Decorated[921]
- Rising One[922]
- Ruler[923]
- She Fills the Forehead of Her Father with Her Beauty[924]
- She Rejoices[925]
- She Who Brightens Up the Two Lands upon Her Rising[926]
- She Who Brightens Up the Two Lands in Her Emergence[927]

---

[914] Leitz, Christian, and Dagmar Budde, et. al. Lexikon der Ägyptischen Götter und Götterbezeichnungen (LGG, OLA 129, Band 8). (Peeters, 2003), 694.

[915] Leitz, Christian, and Dagmar Budde, et. al. Lexikon der Ägyptischen Götter und Götterbezeichnungen (LGG, OLA 129, Band 8). (Peeters, 2003), 694.

[916] Leitz, Christian, and Dagmar Budde, et. al. Lexikon der Ägyptischen Götter und Götterbezeichnungen (LGG, OLA 129, Band 8). (Peeters, 2003), 694.

[917] Leitz, Christian, and Dagmar Budde, et. al. Lexikon der Ägyptischen Götter und Götterbezeichnungen (LGG, OLA 129, Band 8). (Peeters, 2003), 694.

[918] Leitz, Christian, and Dagmar Budde, et. al. Lexikon der Ägyptischen Götter und Götterbezeichnungen (LGG, OLA 129, Band 8). (Peeters, 2003), 694.

[919] Leitz, Christian, and Dagmar Budde, et. al. Lexikon der Ägyptischen Götter und Götterbezeichnungen (LGG, OLA 129, Band 8). (Peeters, 2003), 694.

[920] Leitz, Christian, and Dagmar Budde, et. al. Lexikon der Ägyptischen Götter und Götterbezeichnungen (LGG, OLA 129, Band 8). (Peeters, 2003), 693.

[921] Leitz, Christian, and Dagmar Budde, et. al. Lexikon der Ägyptischen Götter und Götterbezeichnungen (LGG, OLA 129, Band 8). (Peeters, 2003), 694.

[922] Leitz, Christian, and Dagmar Budde, et. al. Lexikon der Ägyptischen Götter und Götterbezeichnungen (LGG, OLA 129, Band 8). (Peeters, 2003), 693.

[923] Leitz, Christian, and Dagmar Budde, et. al. Lexikon der Ägyptischen Götter und Götterbezeichnungen (LGG, OLA 129, Band 8). (Peeters, 2003), 694.

[924] Leitz, Christian, and Dagmar Budde, et. al. Lexikon der Ägyptischen Götter und Götterbezeichnungen (LGG, OLA 129, Band 8). (Peeters, 2003), 694.

[925] Leitz, Christian, and Dagmar Budde, et. al. Lexikon der Ägyptischen Götter und Götterbezeichnungen (LGG, OLA 129, Band 8). (Peeters, 2003), 694.

[926] Leitz, Christian, and Dagmar Budde, et. al. Lexikon der Ägyptischen Götter und Götterbezeichnungen (LGG, OLA 129, Band 8). (Peeters, 2003), 693.

[927] Leitz, Christian, and Dagmar Budde, et. al. Lexikon der Ägyptischen Götter und Götterbezeichnungen (LGG, OLA 129, Band 8). (Peeters, 2003), 693.

- She Who Causes the Plants to Grow[928]
- She Who Makes Everyone to See[929]
- She Who Makes the Food[930]
- She Who Makes Magnificent Things for the Lord of All[931]
- She Who Keeps Her Brother Safe[932]
- She Who Loves Perfection[933]
- She Who is Over the Great Throne[934]
- She Who Prepares the Abundant Grain[935]
- She Who is in the midst of Kom Ombo[936]
- She Who Turns to the Two Mountains with Her Steps[937]
- Two Children[938]
- Two Falcons[939]
- Udjat Eye/Eye of Heru[940]
- Under Whose Speech the King's Decree Comes Out[941]

[928] Leitz, Christian, and Dagmar Budde, et. al. Lexikon der Ägyptischen Götter und Götterbezeichnungen (LGG, OLA 129, Band 8). (Peeters, 2003), 694.
[929] Leitz, Christian, and Dagmar Budde, et. al. Lexikon der Ägyptischen Götter und Götterbezeichnungen (LGG, OLA 129, Band 8). (Peeters, 2003), 694.
[930] Leitz, Christian, and Dagmar Budde, et. al. Lexikon der Ägyptischen Götter und Götterbezeichnungen (LGG, OLA 129, Band 8). (Peeters, 2003), 695.
[931] Leitz, Christian, and Dagmar Budde, et. al. Lexikon der Ägyptischen Götter und Götterbezeichnungen (LGG, OLA 129, Band 8). (Peeters, 2003), 694.
[932] Leitz, Christian, and Dagmar Budde, et. al. Lexikon der Ägyptischen Götter und Götterbezeichnungen (LGG, OLA 129, Band 8). (Peeters, 2003), 694.
[933] Leitz, Christian, and Dagmar Budde, et. al. Lexikon der Ägyptischen Götter und Götterbezeichnungen (LGG, OLA 129, Band 8). (Peeters, 2003), 694.
[934] Leitz, Christian, and Dagmar Budde, et. al. Lexikon der Ägyptischen Götter und Götterbezeichnungen (LGG, OLA 129, Band 8). (Peeters, 2003), 694.
[935] Leitz, Christian, and Dagmar Budde, et. al. Lexikon der Ägyptischen Götter und Götterbezeichnungen (LGG, OLA 129, Band 8). (Peeters, 2003), 694.
[936] Leitz, Christian, and Dagmar Budde, et. al. Lexikon der Ägyptischen Götter und Götterbezeichnungen (LGG, OLA 129, Band 8). (Peeters, 2003), 693.
[937] Leitz, Christian, and Dagmar Budde, et. al. Lexikon der Ägyptischen Götter und Götterbezeichnungen (LGG, OLA 129, Band 8). (Peeters, 2003), 694.
[938] Leitz, Christian, and Dagmar Budde, et. al. Lexikon der Ägyptischen Götter und Götterbezeichnungen (LGG, OLA 129, Band 8). (Peeters, 2003), 694.
[939] Leitz, Christian, and Dagmar Budde, et. al. Lexikon der Ägyptischen Götter und Götterbezeichnungen (LGG, OLA 129, Band 8). (Peeters, 2003), 694.
[940] Leitz, Christian, and Dagmar Budde, et. al. Lexikon der Ägyptischen Götter und Götterbezeichnungen (LGG, OLA 129, Band 8). (Peeters, 2003), 694.

- Uraeus of Light[942]
- Venerable Uraeus[943]
- Who Created Everything[944]
- Who Illuminates the Two Land with Her Rays[945]
- Who Keeps Alive What Exists[946]
- Who is in the Middle of the Palace[947]
- Who Unites with Her Brother[948]
- Whose Defense Against Her Does Not Exist in Heaven or on Earth[949]
- Whose Power is Great Against the Enemies of Her Father[950]
- With the Beautiful Face[951]
- With Great Magic on the Head of Her Father[952]
- With the Sparkling Jewelry[953]
- Without Her Likeness[954]

---

[941] Leitz, Christian, and Dagmar Budde, et. al. Lexikon der Ägyptischen Götter und Götterbezeichnungen (LGG, OLA 129, Band 8). (Peeters, 2003), 694.

[942] Leitz, Christian, and Dagmar Budde, et. al. Lexikon der Ägyptischen Götter und Götterbezeichnungen (LGG, OLA 129, Band 8). (Peeters, 2003), 693.

[943] Leitz, Christian, and Dagmar Budde, et. al. Lexikon der Ägyptischen Götter und Götterbezeichnungen (LGG, OLA 129, Band 8). (Peeters, 2003), 694.

[944] Junker, Hermann. "Der Auszug der Hathor-Tefnut aus Nubien." *Abhandlungen der Preußischen Akademie der Wissenschaften, philosophisch-historische Klasse* (1911), 61.

[945] Leitz, Christian, and Dagmar Budde, et. al. Lexikon der Ägyptischen Götter und Götterbezeichnungen (LGG, OLA 129, Band 8). (Peeters, 2003), 693.

[946] Leitz, Christian, and Dagmar Budde, et. al. Lexikon der Ägyptischen Götter und Götterbezeichnungen (LGG, OLA 129, Band 8). (Peeters, 2003), 694.

[947] Leitz, Christian, and Dagmar Budde, et. al. Lexikon der Ägyptischen Götter und Götterbezeichnungen (LGG, OLA 129, Band 8). (Peeters, 2003), 694.

[948] Leitz, Christian, and Dagmar Budde, et. al. Lexikon der Ägyptischen Götter und Götterbezeichnungen (LGG, OLA 129, Band 8). (Peeters, 2003), 694.

[949] Leitz, Christian, and Dagmar Budde, et. al. Lexikon der Ägyptischen Götter und Götterbezeichnungen (LGG, OLA 129, Band 8). (Peeters, 2003), 694.

[950] Leitz, Christian, and Dagmar Budde, et. al. Lexikon der Ägyptischen Götter und Götterbezeichnungen (LGG, OLA 129, Band 8). (Peeters, 2003), 694.

[951] Leitz, Christian, and Dagmar Budde, et. al. Lexikon der Ägyptischen Götter und Götterbezeichnungen (LGG, OLA 129, Band 8). (Peeters, 2003), 694.

[952] Leitz, Christian, and Dagmar Budde, et. al. Lexikon der Ägyptischen Götter und Götterbezeichnungen (LGG, OLA 129, Band 8). (Peeters, 2003), 694.

[953] Leitz, Christian, and Dagmar Budde, et. al. Lexikon der Ägyptischen Götter und Götterbezeichnungen (LGG, OLA 129, Band 8). (Peeters, 2003), 694.

- Without Whose Knowledge No One Will Enter the Palace[955]

---

[954] Leitz, Christian, and Dagmar Budde, et. al. Lexikon der Ägyptischen Götter und Götterbezeichnungen (LGG, OLA 129, Band 8). (Peeters, 2003), 694.

[955] Leitz, Christian, and Dagmar Budde, et. al. Lexikon der Ägyptischen Götter und Götterbezeichnungen (LGG, OLA 129, Band 8). (Peeters, 2003), 694.

TITLES OF TEFNUT-SEKHMET

- Burning Enemies with Her Burning Breath[956]
- Daughter of Ra in Senmet[957]
- Flame[958]
- Her Majesty Returns to the Land of the Pure Place[959]
- In the Abaton[960]
- In Biggeh[961]
- Great in Millions[962]
- One Who Burns Apep with Her Flame[963]
- One Who Consumes the Enemies with the Burning Breath of Her Mouth[964]
- Powerful[965]
- Powerful in Senmet[966]

---

[956] Inconnu-Bocquillon, Danielle, *Le mythe de la déesse lointaine à Philae, BdE 132*, (Le Caire/Cairo: IFAO, 2001), 83.

[957] Inconnu-Bocquillon, Danielle, *Le mythe de la déesse lointaine à Philae, BdE 132*, (Le Caire/Cairo: IFAO, 2001), 83.

[958] Inconnu-Bocquillon, Danielle, *Le mythe de la déesse lointaine à Philae, BdE 132*, (Le Caire/Cairo: IFAO, 2001), 83.

[959] Inconnu-Bocquillon, Danielle, *Le mythe de la déesse lointaine à Philae, BdE 132*, (Le Caire/Cairo: IFAO, 2001), 83.

[960] Inconnu-Bocquillon, Danielle, *Le mythe de la déesse lointaine à Philae, BdE 132*, (Le Caire/Cairo: IFAO, 2001), 119.

[961] Hoenes, Sigrid-Eike. Untersuchungen zu Wesen und Kult der Göttin Sachmet. (Habelt, 1976), 243.

[962] Siuda, Tamara L. The Ancient Egyptian Daybook. (Stargazer Design, 2016), 198.

[963] Inconnu-Bocquillon, Danielle, *Le mythe de la déesse lointaine à Philae, BdE 132*, (Le Caire/Cairo: IFAO, 2001), 83.

[964] Inconnu-Bocquillon, Danielle, *Le mythe de la déesse lointaine à Philae, BdE 132*, (Le Caire/Cairo: IFAO, 2001), 83.

[965] Inconnu-Bocquillon, Danielle, *Le mythe de la déesse lointaine à Philae, BdE 132*, (Le Caire/Cairo: IFAO, 2001), 83.

[966] Inconnu-Bocquillon, Danielle, *Le mythe de la déesse lointaine à Philae, BdE 132*, (Le Caire/Cairo: IFAO, 2001), 83.

- Regent of the Spirits and Emissaries[967]
- Sekhmet, the Great[968]
- She Will Burst Like Flame to the Sky, Then Her Name Will Be Sopdet[969]
- Sopdet–Sothis or Sirius[970]
- Tefnut in Senmet[971]
- *Uraeus* of Heruakhety[972]
- Venerable[973]
- Who Unites with Her Brother[974]

---

[967] Inconnu-Bocquillon, Danielle, *Le mythe de la déesse lointaine à Philae*, BdE 132, (Le Caire/Cairo: IFAO, 2001), 83.

[968] Inconnu-Bocquillon, Danielle, *Le mythe de la déesse lointaine à Philae*, BdE 132, (Le Caire/Cairo: IFAO, 2001), 119.

[969] Inconnu-Bocquillon, Danielle, *Le mythe de la déesse lointaine à Philae*, BdE 132, (Le Caire/Cairo: IFAO, 2001), 83.

[970] Inconnu-Bocquillon, Danielle, *Le mythe de la déesse lointaine à Philae*, BdE 132, (Le Caire/Cairo: IFAO, 2001), 83.

[971] Inconnu-Bocquillon, Danielle, *Le mythe de la déesse lointaine à Philae*, BdE 132, (Le Caire/Cairo: IFAO, 2001), 119.

[972] Inconnu-Bocquillon, Danielle, *Le mythe de la déesse lointaine à Philae*, BdE 132, (Le Caire/Cairo: IFAO, 2001), 83.

[973] Inconnu-Bocquillon, Danielle, *Le mythe de la déesse lointaine à Philae*, BdE 132, (Le Caire/Cairo: IFAO, 2001), 83.

[974] Inconnu-Bocquillon, Danielle, *Le mythe de la déesse lointaine à Philae*, BdE 132, (Le Caire/Cairo: IFAO, 2001), 119.

Sacred Animals of Tefnut

- Cat
- Cobra
- Female Dorkas Gazelle
- Female Eagle[975]
- Lion
- Lioness
- Snake
- *Uraeus*
- Vulture[976]

---

[975] Spiegelberg, Wilhelm. *Der ägyptische Mythus vom Sonnenauge*. (Georg Olms Verlag, 1917), 28, footnote 11.

[976] Leitz, Christian, and Dagmar Budde, et. al. Lexikon der Ägyptischen Götter und Götterbezeichnungen (LGG, OLA 129, Band 8). (Peeters, 2003), 700.

Sacred Animals of Tefnut-Tasenetnofret

- Falcon[977]

---

[977] Leitz, Christian, and Dagmar Budde, et. al. Lexikon der Ägyptischen Götter und Götterbezeichnungen (LGG, OLA 129, Band 8). (Peeters, 2003), 694.

Identification with Other Gods: Tefnut

- Hethert
- Hethert-Mut
- Khnum-Nebetuu
- Ma'at
- Menhyt
- Menhyt-Nebetuu
- Meskhenet (Birth Goddess)
- Mut
- Nebetuu (Lady of the Primoridal Time)
- Pakhet
- Renenutet
- Repyt—the Lady
- *Ruty*—Pair of Lions with Shu
- Sekhmet
- Shesemtet-Sekhmet
- Tasenetnofret
- Weret Hekau[978]

---

[978] Leitz, Christian, and Dagmar Budde, et. al. <u>Lexikon der Ägyptischen Götter und Götterbezeichnungen (LGG, OLA 129, Band 8).</u> (Peeters, 2003), 702.

Identification with Other Gods: Tefnut-Tasenetnofret

- Raet—Female Ra
- Renenutet
- *Ruty*—Tefnut and Shu as the Two Lions
- Weret Hekau[979]

---

[979] Leitz, Christian, and Dagmar Budde, et. al. <u>Lexikon der Ägyptischen Götter und Götterbezeichnungen (LGG, OLA 129, Band 8).</u> (Peeters, 2003), 695 and 693-694.

Shrine of Tefnut

Iconography

Tefnut is normally shown as a lioness headed woman with a uraeus or a sundisk and uraeus as her crown. Modern devotees can use a generic Sekhmet or lioness statue for Tefnut. Keep in mind that Tefnut's ears are traditionally pointed or square, while Sekhmet's are round. Given that, we can only use what is available to us and if all we can find is a Sekhmet statue to represent Tefnut then that's what we do. You can also commission a Tefnut statue from a sculptor for a reasonable price.

Paintings can also be used. There are paintings of Tefnut available online.

Colors
- Black
- Blue
- Green
- Blue/Green
- Red
- White
- Gold
- Gold and Blue/Silver (with Shu)

Offerings
- Amarula Liqueur
- Beef
- Beer
- Bread

- Caesar Salad
- Chicken
- Chocolate
- Chocolate Milk
- Cookies
- Desserts with Elderflower
- Drinks with Elderflower
- Duck
- Lemonade
- Meat
- Milk
- Peanut Butter Cookies
- Sparkling Wine
- Sweet White Wine
- Tea
- Vanilla Ice Cream
- Vanilla Tea
- Vegetables
- Water

Nonedible Offerings

- Rosewater

Stones

- Amazonite
- Amber
- Apatite
- Aquamarine
- Carnelian
- Malachite
- Labradorite

- Lapis Lazuli
- Turquoise

Symbols

- Clouds
- Cobra
- Full Moon (Hethert-Tefnut)
- Lion
- Lioness
- Menat Necklace
- Rain
- Sistrum
- Sopdet (Sirius)
- Storms
- Sun
- Sunbeams
- Twin Lions (with Shu)
- Venus, the Planet
- Water
- Weather

Family

Father
- Atum
- Ra
- Wesir

Mother
- Aset
- Hethert
- Hethert-Iusaaset
- Iusaaset
- Nit

Husband
- Shu

Siblings
- Ma'at
- Hethert
- Shu

Children with Shu
- Aset
- Geb
- Heru
- Nut

- Wesir

Grandchildren as Tefnut, Mother of Nut
- Aset
- Heru Wer
- Nebet Het
- Set
- Sobek
- Wepwawet
- Wesir

Grandchildren as Tefnut, Mother of Aset
- Amun-Ra
- Amun
- Heru-sa-Aset
- Heru Wer
- Min
- Sobek
- Wepwawet
- Yinepu

Grandchildren as Tefnut, Mother of Wesir
- Amun-Ra
- Amun
- Heru-sa-Aset
- Heru Wer
- Min
- Sekhmet
- Sobek
- Wepwawet
- Yinepu

THE GOD SHU

Titles of Shu

Names in Ancient Egyptian

- *Anhur* (Onuris)—One Who Brings Back the Distant One[980]
- *Ruty*—Twin Lions of the Eastern and Western Horizons (with Tefnut)[981]
- *Soudja-Ba*—Who Causes *Bau* to Flourish[982]

Names in English

- Air is the *Ba* of Shu[983]
- At the Head of All the Gods[984]
- At the Head of Heliopolis[985]
- At the Head of the House of Shu[986]
- At the Head of Pi-Neter[987]
- Arensnuphis at the Head of Nubia[988]

---

[980] Pinch, Geraldine. Egyptian Mythology: A Guide to the Gods, Goddesses and Traditions of Ancient Egypt. (New York: Oxford University Press, 2004), 71.

[981] Tyldesley, Joyce. The Penguin Book of Myths and Legends of Ancient Egypt. (Penguin Books, 2011), 47.

[982] Inconnu-Bocquillon, Danielle, *Le mythe de la déesse lointaine à Philae, BdE 132*, (Le Caire/Cairo: IFAO, 2001), 119. Thank you to Rev. Dr. Tamara L. Siuda for her help with this translation.

[983] De Wit, Constant. *Le rôle et le sens du lion dans l'Égypte ancienne.* (Belgium: E.J. Brill, 1951), 204.

[984] De Wit, Constant. *Le rôle et le sens du lion dans l'Égypte ancienne.* (Belgium: E.J. Brill, 1951), 208.

[985] Sauneron, Serge, *Esna V: Les fêtes religieuses d'Esna aux derniers siècles du paganisme*, (Cairo: IFAO, 1962; 2004), 90.

[986] De Wit, Constant. *Le rôle et le sens du lion dans l'Égypte ancienne.* (Belgium: E.J. Brill, 1951), 207.

[987] Sauneron, Serge, *Esna V: Les fêtes religieuses d'Esna aux derniers siècles du paganisme*, (Cairo: IFAO, 1962; 2004), 89.

[988] Junker, Hermann. "Der Auszug der Hathor-Tefnut aus Nubien." *Abhandlungen der Preußischen Akademie der Wissenschaften, philosophisch-historische Klasse* (1911), 39.

- *Bau* of Heliopolis (with Tefnut)[989]
- Beneficial Heir of His Father[990]
- Both Eyes (with Tefnut)[991]
- Byproduct of Incense[992]
- Child in Mount Pakhou[993]
- Child of Ra[994]
- Children of Heruakhety (with Tefnut)[995]
- Children of the Cobra-Snake (with Tefnut)[996]
- Chosen by the Udjat[997]
- Divine and Sacred Lion of His Father[998]
- Divine *Ka* of the Geat Lion[999]
- Eldest of Ra[1000]
- Eldest Son of Atum[1001]
- Father of Geb[1002]

---

[989] Leitz, Christian, and Dagmar Budde, et. al. <u>Lexikon der Ägyptischen Götter und Götterbezeichnungen (LGG, OLA 129, Band 8).</u> (Peeters, 2003), 699.

[990] Sauneron, Serge, *Esna V: Les fêtes religieuses d'Esna aux derniers siècles du paganisme,* (Cairo: IFAO, 1962; 2004), 358-363.

[991] Siuda, Tamara L. <u>The Ancient Egyptian Daybook.</u> (Stargazer Design, 2016), 155.

[992] Wise, Elliott. "An" Odor of Sanctity": The Iconography, Magic, and Ritual of Egyptian Incense." *Studia Antiqua* 7, no. 1 (2009): 70.

[993] De Wit, Constant. *Le rôle et le sens du lion dans l'Égypte ancienne.* (Belgium: E.J. Brill, 1951), 206.

[994] De Wit, Constant. *Le rôle et le sens du lion dans l'Égypte ancienne.* (Belgium: E.J. Brill, 1951), 208.

[995] Leitz, Christian, and Dagmar Budde, et. al. <u>Lexikon der Ägyptischen Götter und Götterbezeichnungen (LGG, OLA 129, Band 8).</u> (Peeters, 2003), 701.

[996] Merkelbach, Reinhold. *Isis Regina-Zeus Sarapis: die griechisch-ägyptische Religion nach den Quellen dargestellt.* (Walter de Gruyter, 2012), 34.

[997] Siuda, Tamara L. <u>The Ancient Egyptian Daybook.</u> (Stargazer Design, 2016), 210.

[998] De Wit, Constant. *Le rôle et le sens du lion dans l'Égypte ancienne.* (Belgium: E.J. Brill, 1951), 206.

[999] De Wit, Constant. *Le rôle et le sens du lion dans l'Égypte ancienne.* (Belgium: E.J. Brill, 1951), 252.

[1000] De Wit, Constant. *Le rôle et le sens du lion dans l'Égypte ancienne.* (Belgium: E.J. Brill, 1951), 207.

[1001] Sauneron, Serge, *Esna V: Les fêtes religieuses d'Esna aux derniers siècles du paganisme,* (Cairo: IFAO, 1962; 2004), 212-217.

[1002] De Wit, Constant. *Le rôle et le sens du lion dans l'Égypte ancienne.* (Belgium: E.J. Brill, 1951), 207.

- Father of the Gods[1003]
- Father of Nut[1004]
- God of the Four Feathers[1005]
- God of the Horizon[1006]
- Gods Who Created the Primordial Gods (with Tefnut)[1007]
- Good Companion of Tefnut[1008]
- Good Companion of Tefnut in Senmet[1009]
- Great[1010]
- Great God[1011]
- Great Lion[1012]
- Great One Who Was Far Away[1013]
- Great, at the Head of His Country[1014]
- Great Rulers (with Tefnut)[1015]
- Great of Power[1016]

[1003] Sauneron, Serge, *Esna V: Les fêtes religieuses d'Esna aux derniers siècles du paganisme*, (Cairo: IFAO, 1962; 2004), 358-363.

[1004] De Wit, Constant. *Le rôle et le sens du lion dans l'Égypte ancienne*. (Belgium: E.J. Brill, 1951), 207.

[1005] Mancini, Mattia. "Tefnut l'eliopolitana ad Amarna." *Egitto e Vicino Oriente* 39 (2016): 50.

[1006] De Wit, Constant. *Le rôle et le sens du lion dans l'Égypte ancienne*. (Belgium: E.J. Brill, 1951), 223.

[1007] De Wit, Constant. *Le rôle et le sens du lion dans l'Égypte ancienne*. (Belgium: E.J. Brill, 1951), 178.

[1008] De Wit, Constant. *Le rôle et le sens du lion dans l'Égypte ancienne*. (Belgium: E.J. Brill, 1951), 121.

[1009] Junker, Hermann. "Der Auszug der Hathor-Tefnut aus Nubien." *Abhandlungen der Preußischen Akademie der Wissenschaften, philosophisch-historische Klasse* (1911), 38.

[1010] Junker, Hermann. "Der Auszug der Hathor-Tefnut aus Nubien." *Abhandlungen der Preußischen Akademie der Wissenschaften, philosophisch-historische Klasse* (1911), 87.

[1011] Junker, Hermann. "Der Auszug der Hathor-Tefnut aus Nubien." *Abhandlungen der Preußischen Akademie der Wissenschaften, philosophisch-historische Klasse* (1911), 38.

[1012] De Wit, Constant. *Le rôle et le sens du lion dans l'Égypte ancienne*. (Belgium: E.J. Brill, 1951), 252.

[1013] Junker, Hermann. "Der Auszug der Hathor-Tefnut aus Nubien." *Abhandlungen der Preußischen Akademie der Wissenschaften, philosophisch-historische Klasse* (1911), 63.

[1014] Sauneron, Serge, *Esna V: Les fêtes religieuses d'Esna aux derniers siècles du paganisme*, (Cairo: IFAO, 1962; 2004), 89.

[1015] Leitz, Christian, and Dagmar Budde, et. al. Lexikon der Ägyptischen Götter und Götterbezeichnungen (LGG, OLA 129, Band 8). (Peeters, 2003), 701.

- Great of Praise Among the Gods[1017]
- He is for All Men, the Solar Disk We Live On[1018]
- He Who Gives Life to the Gods and Goddesses[1019]
- He Who Makes Light of the Sky After the Night[1020]
- He Who Repels Enemies from His Temple[1021]
- He Who Repels the Enemes of His Father Ra[1022]
- Illuminate Your Temple[1023]
- Image of Ra[1024]
- In His Name of Sopdu, Master of the East[1025]
- In This Place in His Name of Heru Wer[1026]
- *Ka* and *Kat* (life-force/womb) (with Tefnut)[1027]
- King of the Gods[1028]
- Life and Ma'at (Shu and Tefnut, respectively)[1029]

[1016] De Wit, Constant. *Le rôle et le sens du lion dans l'Égypte ancienne.* (Belgium: E.J. Brill, 1951), 121.

[1017] Junker, Hermann. "Der Auszug der Hathor-Tefnut aus Nubien." *Abhandlungen der Preußischen Akademie der Wissenschaften, philosophisch-historisch Klasse* (1911), 63.

[1018] De Wit, Constant. *Le rôle et le sens du lion dans l'Égypte ancienne.* (Belgium: E.J. Brill, 1951), 205.

[1019] De Wit, Constant. *Le rôle et le sens du lion dans l'Égypte ancienne.* (Belgium: E.J. Brill, 1951), 202.

[1020] De Wit, Constant. *Le rôle et le sens du lion dans l'Égypte ancienne.* (Belgium: E.J. Brill, 1951), 204.

[1021] De Wit, Constant. *Le rôle et le sens du lion dans l'Égypte ancienne.* (Belgium: E.J. Brill, 1951), 206.

[1022] De Wit, Constant. *Le rôle et le sens du lion dans l'Égypte ancienne.* (Belgium: E.J. Brill, 1951), 208.

[1023] De Wit, Constant. *Le rôle et le sens du lion dans l'Égypte ancienne.* (Belgium: E.J. Brill, 1951), 205.

[1024] De Wit, Constant. *Le rôle et le sens du lion dans l'Égypte ancienne.* (Belgium: E.J. Brill, 1951), 206.

[1025] De Wit, Constant. *Le rôle et le sens du lion dans l'Égypte ancienne.* (Belgium: E.J. Brill, 1951), 258.

[1026] Gutbub, Adolphe. *Textes fondamentaux de la théologie de Kom Ombo.* (Institut français d'archéologie orientale du Caire, 1973), 108.

[1027] Lekov, Teodor. "The Role of the Ka in the Process of Creation and Birth." *Journal of Egyptological Studies* 4 (2015): 34.

[1028] De Wit, Constant. *Le rôle et le sens du lion dans l'Égypte ancienne.* (Belgium: E.J. Brill, 1951), 208.

[1029] Pinch, Geraldine. Egyptian Mythology: A Guide to the Gods, Goddesses and Traditions of Ancient Egypt. (New York: Oxford University Press, 2004), 64.

- Lion and Lioness (with Tefnut)[1030]
- Lion, Great of Power, Who Presides Over the North[1031]
- Lion on His Sacred Ground[1032]
- Lord of the Abaton[1033]
- Lord of Biggeh[1034]
- Lord of Esna[1035]
- Lord of the Gods[1036]
- Lord of the Holy Island[1037]
- Lord of Ma'at[1038]
- Lord of Ombos[1039]
- Lord of Philae[1040]
- Lord of Sebennytos[1041]
- Lord of the Sky[1042]
- Lord of Xois[1043]

[1030] Sauneron, Serge, *Esna V: Les fêtes religieuses d'Esna aux derniers siècles du paganisme*, (Cairo: IFAO, 1962; 2004), 90. Excerpt from a hymn. Translated by Chelsea Bolton.

[1031] De Wit, Constant. *Le rôle et le sens du lion dans l'Égypte ancienne.* (Belgium: E.J. Brill, 1951), 261. Shu and Arensnuphis.

[1032] De Wit, Constant. *Le rôle et le sens du lion dans l'Égypte ancienne.* (Belgium: E.J. Brill, 1951), 207.

[1033] De Wit, Constant. *Le rôle et le sens du lion dans l'Égypte ancienne.* (Belgium: E.J. Brill, 1951), 263.

[1034] De Wit, Constant. *Le rôle et le sens du lion dans l'Égypte ancienne.* (Belgium: E.J. Brill, 1951), 121.

[1035] Elsayed, Mohammed A. "Remarks on the Concept of Wind in the Texts of the Temple of Esna." *Shedet* 5, no. 5 (2018): 87.

[1036] Junker, Hermann. "Der Auszug der Hathor-Tefnut aus Nubien." *Abhandlungen der Preußischen Akademie der Wissenschaften, philosophisch-historische Klasse* (1911), 68.

[1037] De Wit, Constant. *Le rôle et le sens du lion dans l'Égypte ancienne.* (Belgium: E.J. Brill, 1951), 210.

[1038] Siuda, Tamara L. The Ancient Egyptian Daybook. (Stargazer Design, 2016), 149.

[1039] De Wit, Constant. *Le rôle et le sens du lion dans l'Égypte ancienne.* (Belgium: E.J. Brill, 1951), 223.

[1040] De Wit, Constant. *Le rôle et le sens du lion dans l'Égypte ancienne.* (Belgium: E.J. Brill, 1951), 263.

[1041] De Wit, Constant. *Le rôle et le sens du lion dans l'Égypte ancienne.* (Belgium: E.J. Brill, 1951), 224.

[1042] De Wit, Constant. *Le rôle et le sens du lion dans l'Égypte ancienne.* (Belgium: E.J. Brill, 1951), 207.

- Massacring the Enemies of His Father[1044]
- Master of the Red Crown and the White Crown[1045]
- Master fo the Sky[1046]
- Mighty in Power[1047]
- *Neheh* (Eternal Recurrence) and *Djet* (Eternal Sameness) (Shu and Tefnut)[1048]
- of Heliopolis[1049]
- of Pnubs[1050]
- One Who Attributes the Luminous[1051]
- Offspring of Ra[1052]
- Pacified Her Who is in the Middle of Her Rage (Tefnut)[1053]
- Protector of His Father[1054]
- Resident of the Temple of Victory[1055]
- Regent of the Company of the Gods[1056]

[1043] Ivan Guermeur, Christophe Thiers. Un éloge xoïte de Ptolémée Philadelphe. La stèle BM EA 616. *Bulletin de l'Institut français d'archéologie orientale*, Institut français d'archéologie orientale, 2001, pp.199.

[1044] Sauneron, Serge, *Esna V: Les fêtes religieuses d'Esna aux derniers siècles du paganisme*, (Cairo: IFAO, 1962; 2004), 89.

[1045] De Wit, Constant. *Le rôle et le sens du lion dans l'Égypte ancienne*. (Belgium: E.J. Brill, 1951), 224.

[1046] De Wit, Constant. *Le rôle et le sens du lion dans l'Égypte ancienne*. (Belgium: E.J. Brill, 1951), 224.

[1047] Junker, Hermann. "Der Auszug der Hathor-Tefnut aus Nubien." *Abhandlungen der Preußischen Akademie der Wissenschaften, philosophisch-historische Klasse* (1911), 38.

[1048] Pinch, Geraldine. Egyptian Mythology: A Guide to the Gods, Goddesses and Traditions of Ancient Egypt. (New York: Oxford University Press, 2004), 197.

[1049] Siuda, Tamara L. The Ancient Egyptian Daybook. (Stargazer Design, 2016), 48.

[1050] De Wit, Constant. *Le rôle et le sens du lion dans l'Égypte ancienne*. (Belgium: E.J. Brill, 1951), 263.

[1051] De Wit, Constant. *Le rôle et le sens du lion dans l'Égypte ancienne*. (Belgium: E.J. Brill, 1951), 225.

[1052] Sauneron, Serge, *Esna V: Les fêtes religieuses d'Esna aux derniers siècles du paganisme*, (Cairo: IFAO, 1962; 2004), 358-363.

[1053] Pinch, Geraldine. Egyptian Mythology: A Guide to the Gods, Goddesses and Traditions of Ancient Egypt. (New York: Oxford University Press, 2004), 72.

[1054] Sauneron, Serge, *Esna V: Les fêtes religieuses d'Esna aux derniers siècles du paganisme*, (Cairo: IFAO, 1962; 2004), 364-366.

[1055] De Wit, Constant. *Le rôle et le sens du lion dans l'Égypte ancienne*. (Belgium: E.J. Brill, 1951), 224.

- Regent of Punt[1057]
- Right Eye[1058]
- Right Eye is the Sun[1059]
- Spiritualize the Dead (with Tefnut)[1060]
- Son of Atum[1061]
- Son of Ra[1062]
- Son of Ra in Senmet[1063]
- Souls of Heliopolis (with Ra and Tefnut)[1064]
- Storm of the Half-Light[1065]
- Strong of Arms[1066]
- Supporter of Nut[1067]
- To Cause the Fields to Grow[1068]
- To Cause the Creation of All the Seeds[1069]
- Twins (with Tefnut)[1070]

[1056] De Wit, Constant. *Le rôle et le sens du lion dans l'Égypte ancienne.* (Belgium: E.J. Brill, 1951), 224.

[1057] De Wit, Constant. *Le rôle et le sens du lion dans l'Égypte ancienne.* (Belgium: E.J. Brill, 1951), 120.

[1058] De Wit, Constant. *Le rôle et le sens du lion dans l'Égypte ancienne.* (Belgium: E.J. Brill, 1951), 116.

[1059] Sauneron, Serge, *Esna V: Les fêtes religieuses d'Esna aux derniers siècles du paganisme,* (Cairo: IFAO, 1962; 2004), 212-217.

[1060] De Wit, Constant. *Le rôle et le sens du lion dans l'Égypte ancienne.* (Belgium: E.J. Brill, 1951), 178.

[1061] Siuda, Tamara L. <u>The Ancient Egyptian Daybook</u>. (Stargazer Design, 2016), 290.

[1062] Sauneron, Serge, *Esna V: Les fêtes religieuses d'Esna aux derniers siècles du paganisme,* (Cairo: IFAO, 1962; 2004), 358-363.

[1063] Junker, Hermann. "Der Auszug der Hathor-Tefnut aus Nubien." *Abhandlungen der Preußischen Akademie der Wissenschaften, philosophisch-historische Klasse* (1911), 39.

[1064] Allen, T. G. *The Book of the Dead or Going Forth by Day.* (Chicago: University of Chicago Press, 1974), 93. Spell 115.

[1065] Wise, Elliott. "An" Odor of Sanctity": The Iconography, Magic, and Ritual of Egyptian Incense." *Studia Antiqua* 7, no. 1 (2009): 70.

[1066] De Wit, Constant. *Le rôle et le sens du lion dans l'Égypte ancienne.* (Belgium: E.J. Brill, 1951), 121.

[1067] Faulkner, Raymond O. <u>The Ancient Egyptian Pyramid Texts</u>. (London: Oxford University Press, 1969), 298. PT 689.

[1068] Elsayed, Mohammed A. "Remarks on the Concept of Wind in the Texts of the Temple of Esna." *Shedet* 5, no. 5 (2018): 87. Adapted from, "To cause the field grows".

[1069] Elsayed, Mohammed A. "Remarks on the Concept of Wind in the Texts of the Temple of Esna." *Shedet* 5, no. 5 (2018): 87.

- Twin Lions of the Horizon (with Tefnut)[1071]
- Twin Souls of Them that are in Mendes (with Tefnut)[1072]
- Two *Bau* (with Tefnut)[1073]
- Two Birds (with Tefnut)[1074]
- Two Birds of Ra (with Tefnut)[1075]
- Two Children (with Tefnut)[1076]
- Two Children of Atum (with Tefnut)[1077]
- Two Children of Ra (with Tefnut)[1078]
- Two Children as Eyes (with Tefnut)[1079]
- Two Crocodiles (with Tefnut)[1080]
- Two Disks (with Tefnut)[1081]
- Two Eyes of Heru (with Tefnut)[1082]
- Two Gods (with Tefnut)[1083]

[1070] Tyldesley, Joyce. The Penguin Book of Myths and Legends of Ancient Egypt. (Penguin Books, 2011), 43.

[1071] Pinch, Geraldine. Egyptian Mythology: A Guide to the Gods, Goddesses and Traditions of Ancient Egypt. (New York: Oxford University Press, 2004), 197.

[1072] Allen, T. G. *The Book of the Dead or Going Forth by Day*. (Chicago: University of Chicago Press, 1974), 29. Spell 17: 14.

[1073] Leitz, Christian, and Dagmar Budde, et. al. Lexikon der Ägyptischen Götter und Götterbezeichnungen (LGG, OLA 129, Band 8). (Peeters, 2003), 700.

[1074] Sauneron, Serge, Esna V: Les fêtes religieuses d'Esna aux derniers siècles du paganisme, (Cairo: IFAO, 1962; 2004), 90. Excerpt from a hymn. Translated by Chelsea Bolton.

[1075] Sauneron, Serge, Esna V: Les fêtes religieuses d'Esna aux derniers siècles du paganisme, (Cairo: IFAO, 1962; 2004), 90. Excerpt from a hymn. Translated by Chelsea Bolton.

[1076] Leitz, Christian, and Dagmar Budde, et. al. Lexikon der Ägyptischen Götter und Götterbezeichnungen (LGG, OLA 129, Band 8). (Peeters, 2003), 700.

[1077] Sauneron, Serge, Esna V: Les fêtes religieuses d'Esna aux derniers siècles du paganisme, (Cairo: IFAO, 1962; 2004), 90. Excerpt from a hymn. Translated by Chelsea Bolton.

[1078] Leitz, Christian, and Dagmar Budde, et. al. Lexikon der Ägyptischen Götter und Götterbezeichnungen (LGG, OLA 129, Band 8). (Peeters, 2003), 700.

[1079] Sauneron, Serge, Esna V: Les fêtes religieuses d'Esna aux derniers siècles du paganisme, (Cairo: IFAO, 1962; 2004), 90. Excerpt from a hymn. Leitz, Christian, and Dagmar Budde, et. al. Lexikon der Ägyptischen Götter und Götterbezeichnungen (LGG, OLA 129, Band 8). (Peeters, 2003), 702.

[1080] Sternberg-El Hotabi, Heike., Sternberg, Heike. Mythische Motive und Mythenbildung in den ägyptischen Tempeln und Papyri der griechisch-römischen Zeit. (Germany: Harrassowitz, 1985), 38.

[1081] Leitz, Christian, and Dagmar Budde, et. al. Lexikon der Ägyptischen Götter und Götterbezeichnungen (LGG, OLA 129, Band 8). (Peeters, 2003), 698.

[1082] Leitz, Christian, and Dagmar Budde, et. al. Lexikon der Ägyptischen Götter und Götterbezeichnungen (LGG, OLA 116, Band 7). (Peeters, 2002), 36-37.

- Two Great Ones (with Tefnut)[1084]
- Two Great Gods of Heliopolis (with Tefnut)[1085]
- Two Great Spotted Cats (with Tefnut) [1086]
- Two Lions (with Tefnut)[1087]
- Two Powers (with Tefnut)[1088]
- Two Siblings (with Tefnut)[1089]
- Two Who Come Out of Atum (with Tefnut)[1090]
- When She (Tefnut) Came Back from Bugem, Shu Danced[1091]
- Who Are in Heliopolis (with Tefnut and Atum)[1092]
- Who Brings Wesir to Life[1093]
- Who Brought Back the Eye of Ra (Tefnut)[1094]
- Who Came from Nubia[1095]
- Who Came to Egypt with His Sister Tefnut[1096]

[1083] Leitz, Christian, and Dagmar Budde, et. al. Lexikon der Ägyptischen Götter und Götterbezeichnungen (LGG, OLA 129, Band 8). (Peeters, 2003), 702.

[1084] Leitz, Christian, and Dagmar Budde, et. al. Lexikon der Ägyptischen Götter und Götterbezeichnungen (LGG, OLA 129, Band 8). (Peeters, 2003), 702. From transliteration of the hieroglyphs.

[1085] Leitz, Christian, and Dagmar Budde, et. al. Lexikon der Ägyptischen Götter und Götterbezeichnungen (LGG, OLA 129, Band 8). (Peeters, 2003), 699.

[1086] Pinch, Geraldine. Egyptian Mythology: A Guide to the Gods, Goddesses and Traditions of Ancient Egypt. (New York: Oxford University Press, 2004), 197.

[1087] Pinch, Geraldine. Egyptian Mythology: A Guide to the Gods, Goddesses and Traditions of Ancient Egypt. (New York: Oxford University Press, 2004), 197.

[1088] Leitz, Christian, and Dagmar Budde, et. al. Lexikon der Ägyptischen Götter und Götterbezeichnungen (LGG, OLA 129, Band 8). (Peeters, 2003), 702.

[1089] Pinch, Geraldine. Egyptian Mythology: A Guide to the Gods, Goddesses and Traditions of Ancient Egypt. (New York: Oxford University Press, 2004), 63.

[1090] Leitz, Christian, and Dagmar Budde, et. al. Lexikon der Ägyptischen Götter und Götterbezeichnungen (LGG, OLA 129, Band 8). (Peeters, 2003), 701.

[1091] De Wit, Constant. Le rôle et le sens du lion dans l'Égypte ancienne. (Belgium: E.J. Brill, 1951), 120.

[1092] Allen, T. G. The Book of the Dead or Going Forth by Day. (Chicago: University of Chicago Press, 1974), 200. Spell 182: d.

[1093] De Wit, Constant. Le rôle et le sens du lion dans l'Égypte ancienne. (Belgium: E.J. Brill, 1951), 224.

[1094] De Wit, Constant. Le rôle et le sens du lion dans l'Égypte ancienne. (Belgium: E.J. Brill, 1951), 120.

[1095] Junker, Hermann. "Der Auszug der Hathor-Tefnut aus Nubien." Abhandlungen der Preußischen Akademie der Wissenschaften, philosophisch-historische Klasse (1911), 53.

- Who Comes as a Sweet Wind[1097]
- Who Comes as a Sweet Wind to Make All the Existences Live[1098]
- Who Created Your Beauty (with Tefnut and Atum)[1099]
- Who Has the Power to Grant the Wind[1100]
- Who is in Your Name of Anhur (Onuris)[1101]
- Who Made the Gods, Who Begot the Gods and Established the Gods (wth Tefnut)[1102]
- Who Reduces Your Bodies to Ashes[1103]
- Who Resides in Biggeh[1104]
- Who Sits Within the Divine Eye of His Father[1105]
- Who Strikes Apep[1106]
- Who Strikes People with Rebellious Hearts[1107]
- Who Takes Care of Him Who Has Him Begotten[1108]

[1096] De Wit, Constant. *Le rôle et le sens du lion dans l'Égypte ancienne.* (Belgium: E.J. Brill, 1951), 120.
[1097] Elsayed, Mohammed A. "Remarks on the Concept of Wind in the Texts of the Temple of Esna." *Shedet* 5, no. 5 (2018): 87.
[1098] Elsayed, Mohammed A. "Remarks on the Concept of Wind in the Texts of the Temple of Esna." *Shedet* 5, no. 5 (2018): 87.
[1099] Allen, T. G. The Book of the Dead or Going Forth by Day. (Chicago: University of Chicago Press, 1974), 200. Spell 182: d. I changed "thy" to "your".
[1100] Sauneron, Serge, *Esna V: Les fêtes religieuses d'Esna aux derniers siècles du paganisme,* (Cairo: IFAO, 1962; 2004), 87-90.
[1101] De Wit, Constant. *Le rôle et le sens du lion dans l'Égypte ancienne.* (Belgium: E.J. Brill, 1951), 224.
[1102] Faulkner, Raymond O. The Ancient Egyptian Pyramid Texts. (London: Oxford University Press, 1969), 90. PT 301.
[1103] De Wit, Constant. *Le rôle et le sens du lion dans l'Égypte ancienne.* (Belgium: E.J. Brill, 1951), 206.
[1104] Gaber, Amr. "The Central Hall in the Egyptian Temples of the Ptolemaic Period." (PhD diss., Durham University, 2009), 363.
[1105] De Wit, Constant. *Le rôle et le sens du lion dans l'Égypte ancienne.* (Belgium: E.J. Brill, 1951), 206.
[1106] Sauneron, Serge, *Esna V: Les fêtes religieuses d'Esna aux derniers siècles du paganisme,* (Cairo: IFAO, 1962; 2004), 89.
[1107] Sauneron, Serge, *Esna V: Les fêtes religieuses d'Esna aux derniers siècles du paganisme,* (Cairo: IFAO, 1962; 2004), 364-366.
[1108] Ivan Guermeur, Christophe Thiers. Un éloge xoïte de Ptolémée Philadelphe. La stèle BM EA 616. *Bulletin de l'Institut français d'archéologie orientale,* Institut français d'archéologie orientale, 2001, pp.199.

- Who Yourselves Created Your Godheads and Your Persons (with Tefnut)[1109]
- Whose Body is Youthful as the Two Children of Ra (with Tefnut)[1110]
- Whose Stride is the Length of the Sky[1111]
- Wind of Life[1112]
- With the Strong Arm[1113]
- Yesterday and Tomorrow (with Tefnut)[1114]
- You Who Light Up Hearts[1115]

[1109] Faulkner, Raymond O. The Ancient Egyptian Pyramid Texts. (London: Oxford University Press, 1969), 90. PT 301.

[1110] Leitz, Christian, and Dagmar Budde, et. al. Lexikon der Ägyptischen Götter und Götterbezeichnungen (LGG, OLA 129, Band 8). (Peeters, 2003), 700.

[1111] Pinch, Geraldine. Egyptian Mythology: A Guide to the Gods, Goddesses and Traditions of Ancient Egypt. (New York: Oxford University Press, 2004), 197.

[1112] Sauneron, Serge, Esna V: Les fêtes religieuses d'Esna aux derniers siècles du paganisme, (Cairo: IFAO, 1962; 2004), 90.

[1113] Sauneron, Serge, Esna V: Les fêtes religieuses d'Esna aux derniers siècles du paganisme, (Cairo: IFAO, 1962; 2004), 89.

[1114] Pinch, Geraldine. Egyptian Mythology: A Guide to the Gods, Goddesses and Traditions of Ancient Egypt. (New York: Oxford University Press, 2004), 197.

[1115] Sauneron, Serge, Esna V: Les fêtes religieuses d'Esna aux derniers siècles du paganisme, (Cairo: IFAO, 1962; 2004), 358-363.

Sacred Animals of Shu

- Bird[1116]
- Lion[1117]
- Spotted Cat[1118]

[1116] Sauneron, Serge, *Esna V: Les fêtes religieuses d'Esna aux derniers siècles du paganisme*, (Cairo: IFAO, 1962; 2004), 90.

[1117] Pinch, Geraldine. <u>Egyptian Mythology: A Guide to the Gods, Goddesses and Traditions of Ancient Egypt</u>. (New York: Oxford University Press, 2004), 197.

[1118] Pinch, Geraldine. <u>Egyptian Mythology: A Guide to the Gods, Goddesses and Traditions of Ancient Egypt</u>. (New York: Oxford University Press, 2004), 197.

Identification with Other Gods: Shu

- Arensnuphis[1119]
- Djehuty of Pnubs[1120]
- Heru-Shu[1121]
- Heru Wer-Shu[1122]
- Heru with the Strong Arm[1123]
- Heru Wer[1124]
- Heru Wer in His aspect of Heru, with the Vigorous Arm[1125]
- Khnum-Onuris[1126]
- Khnum-Ra[1127]
- Ptah-Shu[1128]
- Shu-Ra[1129]
- Sopdu[1130]

[1119] Junker, Hermann. "Der Auszug der Hathor-Tefnut aus Nubien." *Abhandlungen der Preußischen Akademie der Wissenschaften, philosophisch-historische Klasse* (1911), 39.

[1120] Junker, Hermann. "Der Auszug der Hathor-Tefnut aus Nubien." *Abhandlungen der Preußischen Akademie der Wissenschaften, philosophisch-historische Klasse* (1911), 53.

[1121] Siuda, Tamara L. <u>The Ancient Egyptian Daybook</u>. (Stargazer Design, 2016), 150-151.

[1122] Gutbub, Adolphe. *Textes fondamentaux de la théologie de Kom Ombo.* (Institut français d'archéologie orientale du Caire, 1973), 323-324.

[1123] Sauneron, Serge, *Esna V: Les fêtes religieuses d'Esna aux derniers siècles du paganisme,* (Cairo: IFAO, 1962; 2004), 358-363.

[1124] Gutbub, Adolphe. *Textes fondamentaux de la théologie de Kom Ombo.* (Institut français d'archéologie orientale du Caire, 1973), 108.

[1125] Gutbub, Adolphe. *Textes fondamentaux de la théologie de Kom Ombo.* (Institut français d'archéologie orientale du Caire, 1973), 108.

[1126] Sauneron, Serge, *Esna V: Les fêtes religieuses d'Esna aux derniers siècles du paganisme,* (Cairo: IFAO, 1962; 2004), 358-363.

[1127] Sauneron, Serge, *Esna V: Les fêtes religieuses d'Esna aux derniers siècles du paganisme,* (Cairo: IFAO, 1962; 2004), 358-363.

[1128] Sauneron, Serge, *Esna V: Les fêtes religieuses d'Esna aux derniers siècles du paganisme,* (Cairo: IFAO, 1962; 2004), 211-212.

[1129] De Wit, Constant. *Le rôle et le sens du lion dans l'Égypte ancienne.* (Belgium: E.J. Brill, 1951), 121.

Symbols of Shu

- Air
- Atmosphere
- Breath
- Clouds
- Four Feathers of Anhur
- Incense
- Mist
- Ostrich Feather
- Scent
- Sky
- Sun
- Sunlight
- Wind

[1130] De Wit, Constant. *Le rôle et le sens du lion dans l'Égypte ancienne.* (Belgium: E.J. Brill, 1951), 258-259.

EPILOGUE

Gods and Goddesses Name List

- Aset, Auset (Isis)
- Bast, Bastet (Ubastis, Bubastis)
- Djehuty, Tehuti (Thoth)
- Hethert, Hetharu, Hwt Hrw (Hathor)
- Heruakhety (Horakhty; Horus of the Two Horizons)
- Heru-pa-Khered (Horus, the Child; Harpocrates)
- Heru-sa-Aset (Horus, son of Isis; Horus, the Younger; Harsiese)
- Heru Wer (Horus, the Great; Horus, the Elder)
- Menhyt (Menhit)
- Mut (Mout; Muth)
- Nebet Het, Nebt-Het, Nebet Hwt (Nephthys)
- Nebetuu (Nebtu)
- Nit, Net (Neith)
- Nut (Nuit)
- Ra, Re
- Ra Heruakhety (Ra Horakhty)
- Sekhmet (Sachmis)
- Serqet, Serket, Selket (Selkis)
- Seshat, Seshet, Sesheta (Sefkhet Abwy)
- Sopdet (Sothis; Sirius)
- Tasenetnofret, Tasenetneferet
- Tefnut, Tefenet (Thphenis)
- Wepwawet, Upwawet, Upuaut (Ophois)
- Wepset, Wepeset
- Wesir, Asar, Ausar (Osiris)
- Yinepu, Anpu, Inpu (Anubis)

Place Name List

- Abaton (Temple of Osiris on Bigeh Island near Philae)
- Abdju (Abydos)
- Bugem (Nubia)
- Djedu (Busiris in Lower Egypt)
- Pilak (Philae)
- Iatdi (Temple of Isis at Dendera)
- Iunet (Tentyris; Dendera)
- Iunu (Heliopolis)
- Kenset (Keneset; Bigeh)
- Khem (Letopolis)
- Per Bast (Bubastis)
- Per-Meru (Komir)
- Per Wesir (Busiris in Middle Egypt; Abusir)
- Senmet (Senmut; Elephantine)
- Tpyhwt (Busiris; Aphroditopolis; Atfih)
- Ta-Senet (Latopolis; Esna)
- Zawty (Lycopolis; Asyut)

Bibliography

Allen, T. G. The Book of the Dead or Going Forth by Day.
Chicago: University of Chicago Press, 1974.

Bergman, Jan. Ich Bin Isis: Studien zum memphitischen
Hintergrund der griechischen Isisaretalogien. Almquist &
Wiksell, Uppsalla, 1968.

Borghouts, Joris Frans, ed. Ancient Egyptian Magical Texts. Vol. 9.
Brill, 1978.

Brand, Peter J., Rosa Erika Feleg and William J. Murnane. The
Great Hypostyle Hall in the Temple of Amun at Karnak: Vol 1,
Part 2: Translation and Commentary. Chicago: Oriental
Institute of the University of Chicago, 2018.

Cauville, Sylvie., Lecler, Alain. Dendara I: Traduction. Belgium:
Peeters, 1998.

Cauville, Sylvie. Dendara II: Traduction. Belgium: Uitgeverij
Peeters, 1999.

Cauville, Sylvie. Dendara V-VI: II: Index Phraseologique. Belgium:
Peeters, 2004.

Cauville, Sylvie. Dendara XV: Traduction: Pronaos de Temple
d'Hathor. Peeters, 2012.

Cauville, Sylvie., Hallof, Jochen., Berg, Hans van den. Le temple de
Dendara: les chapelles osiriennes. Egypt: IFAO, 1997.

Cauville, Sylvie. "Hathor en tous ses noms," in BIFAO 115 (2015):
37-76.

De Wit, Constant. Les Inscriptions du Temple d'Opet a Karnak III:
Traduction integrale des textes rituels-Essai d'interpretation. Bruxelles:
Edition de la Fondation Egyptologique Reine Elisabeth, 1968.

De Wit, Constant. *Le rôle et le sens du lion dans l'Égypte ancienne.* Belgium: E.J. Brill, 1951.

El-Sabban, Sherif. Temple Festival Calendars of Ancient Egypt. Wiltshire: Liverpool University Press, 2000.

Elsayed, Mohammed A. "Remarks on the Concept of Wind in the Texts of the Temple of Esna." *Shedet* 5, no. 5 (2018): 82-95.

El-Tonssy, Mohamed A. "The Goddess Rattawy in the Greco-Roman Temples" الإلهة رعت تاوى فى معابد العصر اليونانى الرومانى. *The Conference Book of the General Union of Arab Archeologists. 15.* (2012), pp. 188-214.

Faulkner, Raymond O. The Ancient Egyptian Pyramid Texts. London: Oxford University Press, 1969.

Franke, Detlef. "Middle Kingdom Hymns and Other Sundry Religious Texts-An Inventory", in Egypt: Temple of the Whole World: Studies in Honour of Jan Assmann. Sibylle Meyer, ed. Brill Academic Publishers, 2004.

Gaber, Amr. "The Central Hall in the Egyptian Temples of the Ptolemaic Period." PhD diss., Durham University, 2009.

Goyon, Jean-Claude. "Inscriptions Tardives Du Temple De Mout à Karnak." *Journal of the American Research Center in Egypt* 20 (1983): 47-61.

Gutbub, Adolphe. *Textes fondamentaux de la théologie de Kom Ombo.* Institut français d'archéologie orientale du Caire, 1973.

Guermeur, Ivan and Christophe Thiers. "Un éloge xoïte de Ptolémée Philadelphe. La stèle BM EA 616". *Bulletin de l'Institut français d'archéologie orientale*, IFAO, 2001, pp.197-219.

Hays, Harold M. "Between identity and agency in ancient Egyptian ritual." Nyord R, Kyolby A (ed.). Leiden, 2009: University Repository: Archaeopress: 15–30. hdl:1887/15716.

Hoenes, Sigrid-Eike. Untersuchungen zu Wesen und Kult der Göttin Sachmet. Habelt, 1976.

Hölbl, Günther. Altägypten im Römischen Reich: Die Tempel des römischen Nubien. Vol. 2. Zabern, 2004.

Husson, Constance. L'offrande du miroir dans les temples égyptiens de l'époque gréco-romaine. France: Audin, 1977.

Inconnu-Bocquillon, Danielle, *Le mythe de la déesse lointaine à Philae*, *BdE 132*, Le Caire/Cairo: IFAO, 2001.

Jasnow, Richard, and Ghislaine Widmer, eds. Illuminating Osiris: Egyptological Studies in Honor of Mark Smith. Georgia: Lockwood Press, 2017. http://www.jstor.org/stable/j.ctvvnd2x.

Junker, Hermann. "Der Auszug der Hathor-Tefnut aus Nubien." *Abhandlungen der Preußischen Akademie der Wissenschaften, philosophisch-historische Klasse* (1911), pp. 1-89.

Junker, Hermann. Die Onurislegende. Vol. 59. Hölder, 1917.

Joyful in Thebes: Egyptological Studies in Honor of Betsy M. Bryan. United States: Lockwood Press, 2015.

Kaper, Olaf E., and Oe Kaper. The Egyptian God Tutu: a study of the sphinx-god and master of demons with a corpus of monuments. Peeters Publishers, 2003.

Kockelmann, Holger and Erich Winter, *Philae III: Die Zweite Ostkolonnade des Tempels der Isis in Philae. (CO II und CO II K)*, (Verlag der Osterreichischen Akademie der Wissenschaften/Austrian Academy of Sciences, 2016.

Labrique, Françoise. Stylistique et théologie à Edfou: le rituel de l'offrande de la campagne: étude de la composition. Belgium: Peeters, 1992.

Lafont, Julie. "Consommation et proscription du miel en Égypte ancienne. Quand bj.t devient bw.t," in *BIFAO 116* (2016), p. 97-122.

Leitz, Christian, and Dagmar Budde, et. al. Lexikon der Ägyptischen Götter und Götterbezeichnungen (LGG, OLA 116, Band 7). Peeters, 2002.

Leitz, Christian, and Dagmar Budde, et. al. Lexikon der Ägyptischen Götter und Götterbezeichnungen (LGG, OLA 129, Band 8). Peeters, 2003.

Leitz, Christian. "Der grosse Repithymnus im Tempel von Athribis." In "Parcourir l'éternité", Hommages à Jean Yoyotte Bd. 2 (Bibliothèque de l'École des Hautes Études, Sciences Religieuses 156), Zivie-Coche, Christiane und Guermeur, Ivan (Hg.), (Turnhout 2012), 757-775.

Lekov, Teodor. "The Role of the Ka in the Process of Creation and Birth." *Journal of Egyptological Studies* 4 (2015): 31-48.

Lesko, Barbara. The Great Goddesses of Egypt. Oklahoma: University of Oklahoma Press, 1999.

Mancini, Mattia. "Tefnut l'eliopolitana ad Amarna." *Egitto e Vicino Oriente* 39 (2016): 45-55.

Marín, Antonio Hernández. "Las inscripciones de Mut en el templo de Debod." *Boletín de la Asociación Española de Egiptología* 10 (2000): 179-192.

Merkelbach, Reinhold. *Isis Regina-Zeus Sarapis: die griechisch-ägyptische Religion nach den Quellen dargestellt.* Walter de Gruyter, 2012.

Müller, Dieter. Ägypten und die griechischen Isis-Aretalogien. Vol. 53, no. 1. Akademie-Verlag, 1961.

Nyord, Rune, and Kim Ryholt, eds. Lotus and Laurel: Studies on Egyptian Language and Religion in Honour of Paul John Frandsen. Vol. 39. Museum Tusculanum Press, 2015.

Piehl, Karl. Inscriptions hiéroglyphiques recueillies en Égypte. Germany: n.p., 1890.

Pinch, Geraldine. Egyptian Mythology: A Guide to the Gods, Goddesses and Traditions of Ancient Egypt. New York: Oxford University Press, 2004.

Prada, Luigi. "Divining Grammar and Defining Foes: Linguistic Patterns of Demotic Divinatory Handbooks (with Special Reference to P. Cairo CG 50138-41 and a Note on the Euphemsic Use of *ḥft* Enemy," in Jasnow, Richard, and Ghislaine Widmer, eds. Illuminating Osiris: Egyptological Studies in Honor of Mark Smith. Georgia: Lockwood Press, 2017.

Preys, René. *Les complexes de la Demeure du Sistre et du Trône de Rê: théologie et décoration dans le temple d'Hathor à Dendera.* Vol. 106. Peeters Publishers, 2002.

Preys, René. "Le mythe de la Lointaine: Lionne dangereuse et déesse bénéfique." In *Sphinx: Les gardiens de l'Egypte*, pp. 141-151. Fonds Mercator, 2006.

Reynolds, James Brown. "Sex Morals and the Law in Ancient Egypt and Babylon", in *Journal of the American Institute of Criminal Law and Criminology.* United States: The Institute, 1915.

Richter, Barbara A. The Theology of Hathor of Dendera: Aural and Visual ScrIbal Techniques in the Per-Wer Sanctuary. Lockwood Press, 2016.

Richter, Barbara A. "On the Heels of the Wandering Goddess: The Myth and the Festival at the Temples of the Wadi el-Hallel and Dendera." Dolinska, Monika and Beinlich, Horst (eds.) 8. Ägyptologische Tempeltagung: interconnections between temples : Warschau, 22.-25. September 2008. Germany: Harrassowitz, 2010: 155-186.

Sauneron, Serge, *Esna V: Les fêtes religieuses d'Esna aux derniers siècles du paganisme*, Cairo: IFAO, 1962; 2004.

Sayed, Ramadan. La déesse Neith de Saïs. Egypt: Institut français d'archéologie orientale du Caire, 1982.

Spiegelberg, Wilhelm. *Der ägyptische Mythus vom Sonnenauge.* Georg Olms Verlag, 1917.

Stadler, Martin Andreas. Théologie et culte au temple de Soknopaios: Etudes sur la Religion d'un Village Egyptien Pendant l'Epoque Romaine. Paris: Cybele, 2017.

Sternberg-El Hotabi, Heike., Sternberg, Heike. Mythische Motive und Mythenbildung in den ägyptischen Tempeln und Papyri der griechisch-römischen Zeit. Germany: Harrassowitz, 1985.

Strandberg, Åsa. The Gazelle in Ancient Egyptian Art: Image and Meaning. Sweden: University of Uppsala. Department of Archaeology and Ancient History, 2009.

Tobin, Vincent Arieh. <u>Theological Principles of Egyptian Religion</u>. Vol. 59. Lang, Peter, Publishing Incorporated, 1989.

Tyldesley, Joyce. <u>The Penguin Book of Myths and Legends of Ancient Egypt</u>. Penguin Books, 2011.

Verhoeven, Ursula. "Eine Vergewaltigung? Vom Umgang mit einer Textstelle des Naos von El Arish (Tefnut-Studien I)." <u>Religion und Philosophie im Alten Ägypten, Festgabe für Philippe Derchain, Orientalia Lovaniensia Analecta 39</u>, U. Verhoeven, E. Graefe (Hg.), Leuven 1991, 319-330.

Von Lieven, Alexandra. "Antisocial Gods? On the Transgression of Norms in Ancient Egyptian Mythology," in Nyord, Rune, and Kim Ryholt, eds. <u>Lotus and Laurel: Studies on Egyptian Language and Religion in Honour of Paul John Frandsen</u>. Vol. 39. (Museum Tusculanum Press, 2015), 181-207.

West, Stephanie. "The Greek version of the legend of Tefnut." *The Journal of Egyptian Archaeology* 55, no. 1 (1969): 161-183.

Wilkinson, Richard H. <u>The Complete Gods and Goddesses of Ancient Egypt</u>. New York: Thames and Hudson, 2003.

Wise, Elliott. "An Odor of Sanctity": The Iconography, Magic, and Ritual of Egyptian Incense." *Studia Antiqua* 7, no. 1 (2009): 67-80.

About the Author

Chelsea Luellon Bolton has a BA and MA in Religious Studies from the University of South Florida. She is the author of *Lady of Praise, Lady of Power: Ancient Hymns of the Goddess Aset*; *Queen of the Road: Poetry of the Goddess Aset*; and *Magician, Mother and Queen: A Research Paper on the Goddess Aset*. Her other books are *Lord of Strength and Power: Ancient Hymns for Wepwawet* and *Sun, Star and Desert Sand: Poems for the Egyptian Gods*. She is the editor and a contributor of the anthology *She Who Speaks Through Silence: An Anthology for Nephthys*. Her other latest books are *Mother of Magic: Ancient Hymns for Aset*; *Flaming Lioness: Ancient Hymns for Egyptian Goddesses*; and *Lady of the Temple: Ancient Hymns for Nephthys*. Her poetry has been previously published in various anthologies. You can find more of her work at her blog address: http://fiercelybrightone.com

Website:
https://fiercelybrightone.com/

Other Books by Chelsea Luellon Bolton

Ancient Hymns Collections
Lady of Praise, Lady of Power: Ancient Hymns of the Goddess Aset.
Mother of Magic: Ancient Hymns for Aset.
Lady of the Temple: Ancient Hymns for Nephthys.
Lady of Water and Flame: Ancient Hymns for Tefnut.
Solar Lioness: Ancient Hymns for Sekhmet.
Mother of Writing: Ancient Hymns for Seshat.
Mother of Mothers: Ancient Hymns for Mut.
Lord of Strength and Power: Ancient Hymns for Wepwawet.
Flaming Lioness: Ancient Hymns for Egyptian Goddesses.
Two Horizons: Ancient Hymns for Egyptian Gods.
Beauty and Strength: Ancient Hymns for Egyptian Gods.

Anthologies
Queen of the Hearth: An Anthology for Frigga.
She Who Speaks Through Silence: An Anthology for Nephthys.
Solar Flares and Sunbeams: An Anthology for Ra.
Lord of the Ways: An Anthology for Wepwawet.
Mother of Nine: An Anthology for Oya.
Sweet of Love: An Anthology for Bast and Bast-Mut.
Lady of Arrows: An Anthology for Neith.
Thrice Great Goddess: An Anthology for Aset.

Research Papers
Magician, Mother and Queen: A Research Paper on the Goddess Aset.

Modern Poetry
Queen of the Road: Poetry of the Goddess Aset.
Divine Words, Divine Praise: Poetry for the Divine Powers.
Divine Beings, Earthly Praise: Poems for Divine Powers.
Sun, Star and Desert Sand: Poems for the Egyptian Gods.
River, Star and Sky: Poems for the Egyptian Gods.

Made in the USA
Columbia, SC
15 December 2024

49326100R00126